YORK FILM NOTES

Stagecoach

Director
John Ford

Note by Elizabeth Bowen

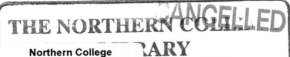

Longman

York Press

BARNSLEY

York Press
322 Old Brompton Road, London SW5 9JH

Pearson Education Limited
Edinburgh Gate, Harlow, Essex CM20 2JE, United Kingdom
Associated companies, branches and representatives throughout
the world

Stills © United Artists, courtesy Kobal
Screenplay reproduced by kind permission of Castle Hill Productions

First published 2000

ISBN 0-582-43187-5

Designed by Vicki Pacey
Phototypeset by Gem Graphics, Trenance, Mawgan Porth, Cornwall
Colour reproduction and film output by Spectrum Colour
Printed in Malaysia, KVP

contents

background 5

trailer 5 key players' biographies 9
reading stagecoach 6 director as auteur 14

narrative & form 17

narrative theory 17 narrative deconstruction 20

style 27

set design & setting 27 special effects 32
costume & make-up 30 sound effects: musical
lighting 30 score 33
cinematography 31 textual ownership &
colour/black & white 32 textual remakes 39

contexts 41

ideology 41 genre 67
character representation 42 production history 68
cultural contexts 62 industrial 70
filmography: intertextual audience 72
motifs 65

bibliography 75
filmography 78
cinematic terms 80
credits 84

author of this note Elizabeth Bowen is currently lecturer in Communication, Media and Theatre Studies at Doncaster College Sixth Form Centre. Her degree from Goldsmiths' College, University of London, was consolidated in postgraduate studies at Leeds University (MA Communication Studies) which resulted in a multidisciplinary thesis centring on the Hollywood film industry. Publications include a case study on applying the internet to the media curriculum in *Snapshots of Innovation* published by British Educational Communications and Technology Agency (1998). Elizabeth also co-delivered a workshop on teaching gangster texts at the BFI Media Studies Conference (South Bank Centre, 1999).

STAGECOACH

background

trailer *p5*   **reading Stagecoach** *p6*   **key players' biographies** *p9*
director as auteur *p14*

trailer

CRITICAL REVIEWS

But for Ford himself and for Merian Cooper in their dispute with Selznick, 'classic' meant something more immediate, meant it would have class – as *Hollywood Reporter* astutely put it – 'One swellegant Western that even the carriage trade will go for.' A film that would not be a Western at all in the limited industry meaning of the term, all action and no talk, a shoot 'em up, but rather a film of universal and perennial appeal.

Edward Buscombe, Stagecoach, p. 88

The *Box Office* review of 11 February 1939 proclaimed the film as 'spectacular for the production scope with which Walter Wanger has endowed it, the majestic scenic backgrounds furnished by Monument Valley, Ariz., the thrilling chases and action footage, and superior photography, here is a 'super-Western' which will find its best market among action addicts. The picture's natural lustre and sweep is dimmed by a faltering, loosely-knit story and the interpretation of too many extraneous situations not germane to the general motivation and theme. The cast is large and competent, with acting honors rather impartially distributed because no part is built to be dominant. Merchandised with stress on the action entertainment elements, the feature will, quite probably, ride through most of its showings with profitable cash drawer records. John Ford directed.'

The review concluded with a number of 'catchlines': 'Life and Death, Adventure and Romance, on the Old Lordsburg Trail ... Blazing a Path Through the Pioneer West ... Come Along for the Most Thrilling Ride of Your Life ... Aboard a Stagecoach Pounding Its Way Through America's Historic Badlands.'

'John Ford in peak form'

In *New York Times* of 3 March 1939 Frank S. Nugent, later to script *Fort Apache* and other Westerns for Ford, wrote:

> John Ford has swept aside ten years of artifice and talkie compromise and has made a motion picture that wings a song of camera. It moves, and how beautifully it moves, across the plains of Arizona, skirting the sky-reaching mesas of Monument Valley, beneath the piled-up cloud banks which every photographer dreams about ... Mr Ford is not one of your subtle directors, suspending sequences on the wink of an eye or the precisely calculated gleam of a candle in a mirror. He prefers the broadest canvas, the brightest colors, the widest brush and the boldest possible strokes. He hews to the straight narrative line with the well-reasoned confidence of a man who has seen that narrative succeed before. He takes no shadings from his characters; either they play it straight or they don't play at all. He likes his language simple and he doesn't want too much of it. When his Redskins bite the dust, he expects to hear the thud and see the dirt spurt up. Above all, he likes to have things happen in the open, where his camera can keep them in view ... This is one stagecoach that's powered by a Ford.

Variety of 8 February 1939 referred to the text as 'a sweeping and powerful drama of the American frontier' which 'displays potentialities that can easily drive it through as one of the surprise big grossers of the year. Without strong marquee names, picture nevertheless presents wide range of exploitation to attract, and will carry far through word-of-mouth after it gets rolling. Directorially, production is John Ford in peak form.'

All the above quotations are taken from Stagecoach by E. Buscombe.

reading stagecoach

The peak year for the productions of Westerns was 1925, when two hundred and twenty-seven were made. *Stagecoach* was produced thirteen years later, and to classify it as simply 'a Western' requires immediate clarification.

different interpretations

When released in 1939, the film was termed a melodrama in the trade press and not a Western. Ford defined the text as a 'classic Western' indicating an intention to rework the established format of existing films and create something new.

This is referred to as a hybrid genre which partly explains the contradictory position of Ford as a director. In one sense the director and his text resist straightforward taxonomy, as critical analyses in this Note will show.

It is difficult to pigeonhole Ford as only a studio Hollywood director creating a mass popular text which the public will want to consume and the industry will wish to garland with academy awards. Stagecoach easily achieves this status and Ford's merit as the director responsible is fully acknowledged.

The difficulty of labelling Ford and his text on these terms alone stems from the fact that the film is also read as a text which espouses Ford's personal beliefs and opinions, resisting the studio line posited in Hollywood at the time.

Ford has therefore been granted a directorial auteur status.

In relation to this, the text is equally revered as a stylistic masterpiece which has proved seminal in advancing technological stunts and film grammar of its time. It has also functioned as a legacy text, inspiring generations of subsequent film practitioners globally. Stagecoach can equally be considered in the light of these secondary characteristics which will be discussed in detail in subsequent textual analysis.

The very essence and textual appeal of Stagecoach for a student lie in its presentation of boundless possibilities of interpretation for the viewer, combining the familiar and the unexpected. Ford offers his vision of a 'classic Western' drawing on established films and associations which his contemporary target audience would understand. He then uses this framework to superimpose his own vision of America's West, creating something new as a result.

In order to contextualise Stagecoach it is important to provide some general background about the setting of the Western. Western films tend to be historically set after the American Civil War of 1861–5, in the period

1865–90. *Stagecoach* subscribes to this pattern. It draws upon the realities of North American history of the nineteenth century which tend to be dramatically re-created as follows:

■ Distance: In 1848 settlers reached the Pacific coast, and the migration of white Americans during this period took place after the discovery of gold in California. Travel over long distances was not easy at this time. The terrain which people had to cross was particularly unfriendly and there was the added threat from the indigenous Indian population.

■ Industrial expansion: America's 'natural' landscape was changing as a result of railway construction across the continent and developments in communications technology, notably the telegraph.

■ Indian resistance: The invasion of 'white people's' technology and their claim to land damaged the Indian reservations and buffalo settlements which were destroyed as a result of the industrial expansion mentioned above. Clashes took place between white American settlers and Indian communities.

■ The professional cowboy: Cowboys came to play an important part in the history of the West. Their duties involved driving the cattle from the plains to the railroad tracks. Disputes occurred between the cowboys and the urban settlers over the use and ownership of land. Some wanted an open range to graze their cattle and develop their homesteads whilst others wanted to section their property rigidly and fence off their farms.

■ Contemporary America: The setting of *Stagecoach* is important formatively as it is linked to a period in America's history when geographically, politically and socially it was organising itself into the modern nation of today.

These context headings should be remembered when viewing *Stagecoach*. Their purpose will be evident in the subsequent close critical examination.

key players' biographies

The credited members of the cast featured in the biographies of key players are:

Claire Trevor –	Dallas
John Wayne –	Henry, the Ringo Kid
Andy Devine –	Buck, the Stagecoach Driver
John Carradine –	Mr Hatfield
Thomas Mitchell –	Doc Josiah Boone
Louise Platt –	Lucy Mallory
George Bancroft –	Curley Wilcox
Donald Meek –	Mr Samuel Peacock
Berton Churchill –	Mr Elswood Henry Gatewood
Tim Holt –	Lieutenant Blanchard

JOHN WAYNE: 'THE RINGO KID'

John Wayne has become a Hollywood icon. This status rests on his ability to convey in his roles American masculine individualism within the Western genre. Wayne's off screen/on screen star personae increasingly merged in later life as he became inextricably linked with right-wing American values.

Born Marion Michael Morrison, he played football for University of Southern California (USC) and held several behind-the-scenes jobs at Fox Studios before appearing in the late 1920s in a series of unmemorable small roles. The famous partnership with director John Ford, who had befriended 'Duke' Wayne when their film careers met, gained Wayne the lead in Raoul Walsh's 1930 Western epic, *The Big Trail* (1930).

Stardom did not come at once and Wayne spent the rest of the decade appearing in a series of low-budget Western pictures with fast shooting schedules which did little to sharpen his acting skills. Despite these early career difficulties, Wayne gained a reputation for asserting a calm authority. His impressive physical presence was seen to advantage on the screen which stressed Wayne's stature and commanding stance.

biographies background

John Ford gave Wayne his pivotal career break in 1939 by casting him as the Ringo Kid in *Stagecoach* (see Contexts: Production history). During the Second World War Wayne was granted exemption from military duty on medical grounds. To contribute towards the American war effort Wayne utilised film to project his military ideal. Wartime releases such as *Flying Tigers* (1942), *The Fighting Seabees* (1944), and *Back To Bataan* (1945) placed Wayne squarely in the larger-than-life, heroic mould (see Contexts: Character representation).

Wayne's final movies established him as an actor of merit. Consequently he rose in status beyond a walk-on star who could fill the screen to a screen performer with gravity. Howard Hawks emphasised the wilful side of Wayne's screen persona, taking it to extremes in *Red River* (1948). Two other John Ford films from the period gave Wayne the opportunity for greater depth – *Fort Apache* (1948) and *She Wore a Yellow Ribbon* (1949) – the latter a particularly moving portrait of a man and an era reaching a turning point.

When he was awarded the 1969 Best Actor Oscar for *True Grit* (1969), many film critics regarded this as a lifetime achievement award in disguise. This judgement was due to the lighthearted ease of Wayne's performance.

CLAIRE TREVOR: 'DALLAS'

Claire Trevor gained a theatrical reputation on the New York stage. Her progression from Brooklyn to Vitaphone was made in the early 1930s. She made a series of feature film debuts in 1933, and was quickly typecast within the Hollywood system as a hardened but sympathetic female victim or a gangster's moll in a host of B movies (see Contexts: Character representation). She gained critical acclaim as Dallas in *Stagecoach* for which she received star top billing.

The 1940s and 1950s witnessed Trevor consolidating her early career successes in films such as *Key Largo* (1948) and *The High and the Mighty* (1954). She also employed her screen talents in a number of TV productions, receiving an Emmy for a Best Supporting Actress performance opposite Fredric March in *Dodsworth* (1956). Claire Trevor is an actress noted for her ability to express emotion without words, imbuing her roles with a tragic quality that suited the melodramatic mood of 1930s and 1940s Hollywood.

LOUISE PLATT: 'LUCY MALLORY'

Louise Platt trod the Broadway boards and made a name for herself there before transferring her talents onto the big screen. Lucy Mallory remains her most significant screen role. Interestingly, she was the first actress to test for the coveted Scarlett O'Hara role in *Gone with the Wind*.

ANDY DEVINE: 'BUCK, THE STAGECOACH DRIVER'

Devine transferred his on-pitch college football skills to on-screen personae when he arrived in Hollywood in 1926. He served his apprenticeship playing a variety of bit parts in lighthearted silent pictures before progressing to talkies. A childhood accident had given him a distinctive raspy voice which was initially deemed unsuitable for talking films. His voice later became an asset when coupled with his rotund appearance which lent itself to comic roles. Devine became a comic sidekick for Roy Rogers and other screen cowboys in numerous Westerns. In the early 1950s he played Jingles, Guy Madison's sidekick, in the TV series 'Wild Bill Hickok'.

THOMAS MITCHELL: 'DOC JOSIAH BOONE'

Thomas Mitchell established a reputation as a fine character actor. This reputation spanned the American stage and screen alike. Before becoming an actor he worked as reporter on the *Elizabeth Daily Journal*. He started writing plays then, some of which were produced on stage and adapted to films. His play *Little Accident*, which he wrote in collaboration with Floyd Dell, was adapted to the screen in 1930 and 1939, and again in 1944 as *Casanova Brown*. In 1934 Thomas Mitchell collaborated on the screenplay of *All of Me*.

With the exception of a single appearance in a silent film of the 1920s, he remained a stage actor until the mid 1930s, when he turned his attention almost exclusively to the screen. He won an Academy Award as best supporting actor for his memorable portrayal of the tipsy Doc Boone in *Stagecoach* (see Contexts: Character representation). That same year he appeared as Scarlett O'Hara's father in *Gone with the Wind* (1939) and played another memorable role in *Only Angels Have Wings* (1939). This was an amazing year for Mitchell who appeared not only in *Stagecoach* and *Gone with the Wind*, but also in *Mr Smith Goes to Washington* and *The Hunchback of Notre Dame*.

GEORGE BANCROFT: 'CURLEY WILCOX'

Bancroft commenced his stage career as a 'black face entertainer' in minstrel shows. His New York stage performances included musical comedy routines. His screen debut was *The Journey's End* (1921). This brought him to the attention of Paramount, resulting in a role in *Code of the West* (1925), and of the director James Cruze, who cast him in *The Pony Express* (1925).

Owing to his strong physical build, Bancroft was routinely cast as a heavy with a slick villainous acting style. By casting him as a tough 'good guy' in leads and supporting parts John Ford enabled Bancroft to demonstrate his full dramatic range (see Contexts: Character representation).

BERTON CHURCHILL: 'MR ELSWOOD HENRY GATEWOOD'

Churchill served a political apprenticeship as a labour leader. He was president of New York's Press Feeders' Union and a member of Tammany Hall's Board of Speakers. He began playing character parts on Broadway around 1910.

After occasional appearances in silent films, his main screen career developed with the advent of sound. Churchill acted in some one hundred and fifty pictures in ten years. In 1932 alone he appeared in more than thirty films, typically as a sour businessman (see Contexts: Character representation) or leading small-town citizen, and also as the Judge in *I am a Fugitive from a Chain Gang* (1932).

FRANCIS FORD: 'BILLY PICKETT'

Born Francis O'Feeney (O'Fearna), the older brother and mentor of John Ford, Francis Ford began his career as an actor with various stock companies and made occasional Broadway appearances. He entered films as an actor with Edison in 1907, later moving to Vitagraph and finally to Universal.

In 1913 he became a director of shorts and action serials, in many of which he also starred, for instance as Colonel Custer in *Custer's Last Stand* (1912). Ford, who had changed his surname while a stage actor, gave his brother John his adopted surname and first opportunity in films. It was as Francis's assistant that John Ford learned the rudiments of film technique. Years later, when Francis's career as director waned, the roles were reversed, Francis becoming a frequent character player in John's pictures as well as in those of other directors, typically as a grizzly old-timer.

JOHN CARRADINE: 'MR HATFIELD'

Born Richmond Reed Carradine, he first acted under the name of John Peter Richmond, changing it in 1939 to John Carradine. Carradine made a name for himself as a supporting player appearing in ten John Ford films, including the 1940 classic *The Grapes of Wrath*. Carradine was also a keen Shakespearean stage actor, and his habit of reciting soliloquies while walking in public earned him the nickname 'Bard of the Boulevard'. Father of four current acting Carradines: David, Robert, Keith and Bruce.

DONALD MEEK: 'MR SAMUEL PEACOCK'

Donald Meek's appearance – slight, bald – made him instantly recognisable. His name appropriately indicates the many timid roles in which he was so often cast. He featured in a number of stage productions on Broadway and played McCoy in *Jesse James* (1939).

TIM HOLT: 'LIEUTENANT BLANCHARD'

The son of Jack Holt and brother of Jennifer Holt and David Holt, he appeared as a child in several of his famous father's silent films. He later specialised in playing juveniles and boyish Western heroes in numerous B movies, occasionally getting meatier parts in high-quality films, like Orson Welles's *The Magnificent Ambersons* (1942). Probably the most notable role of his career was that of Curtin, Humphrey Bogart's conscientious partner, in John Huston's *The Treasure of the Sierra Madre* (1948) (in which his father played a bit part). He retired from the screen to go into business in the mid 50s.

ELVIRA RIOS: 'YAKIMA'

A Mexican better known in her native land as a singer than as an actress, her only other Hollywood appearance was as Rosa in *Tropic Holiday* (1938), a Paramount Latin American musical confection of 1938 featuring Tito Guizar, and including Dorothy Lamour and Ray Milland. It is significant that the female 'other' (see Contexts: Character representation) is created by Hollywood using an established 'popular cultural other' anew within their institutional context.

director as auteur

John Ford was born Sean Aloysius O'Fearna, and was also known as Sean Aloysius O'Feeney. In the early feature films he directed his name is given in the credits as Jack Ford.

In the early days of film making, his older brother Francis moved to Hollywood to work for Universal Pictures and John joined him in 1914, serving his apprenticeship as a moviemaker during the formative period of Hollywood's classical era. By 1917 Ford was promoted to contract director, making Westerns which regularly featured Harry Carey.

John Ford moved to the Fox studio in 1921 and established his reputation with such films as the Western spectacular *The Iron Horse* (1924). In his silent films, Ford composed images with a formality and a symmetry that valued order; even at this stage, he had the reputation of a Hollywood master and his experimentation with film methods helped to create his status as an auteur.

Although best known for his Westerns such as the landmark *Stagecoach* (1939), Ford worked in many other genres throughout his long career. Early in the 1930s he directed Fox's top comedy star Will Rogers in *Dr Bull* (1933), *Judge Priest* (1934) and *Steamboat 'Round The Bend* (1935).

The Informer (1935), a drama of the Irish rebellion, won him the first of four Academy Awards for his direction. Critically, the film has been retrospectively dismissed as stylistically cumbersome and thematically didactic, especially when compared to the vibrancy of *The Quiet Man* (1952), an unpretentious film about an Irish-American returning to settle in his native land. Ford also dealt with American history in *The Prisoner of Shark Island* (1936), *Young Mr Lincoln* (1939), *Drums along the Mohawk* (1939) and *The Grapes of Wrath* (1940).

After the Second World War Ford made some of the best Westerns ever to come out of Hollywood, including *She Wore a Yellow Ribbon* (1949), *Wagon Master* (1950), *The Searchers* (1956) and *The Man Who Shot Liberty Valance* (1962). In creating the archetypal shootout pattern for the genre in *My Darling Clementine* (1946), Ford focused on the classic cinematic shootout, the famous final gunfight at the OK Corral, where Wyatt Earp (Henry Fonda) and his brothers avenge the murder of their youngest brother.

Against the harsh background of the Monument Valley, Ford had the Earps joining forces with Easterner Doc Holliday (Victor Mature) to rid Tombstone of the evil Clantons and bring civilisation to the town. In reshaping these familiar features, Ford demonstrated that Hollywood genre films could be transformed into complex artefacts of popular culture and history. Monument Valley which was first used as the location in *Stagecoach* becomes an inspiration for Ford and a signifier for the viewers indicating that they are seeing a John Ford Western.

Ford's postwar Westerns examined all facets of the settling of the West. He began with optimism shared by *My Darling Clementine* and *She Wore a Yellow Ribbon*, and ended with a close examination of the dark side of destiny in *The Man Who Shot Liberty Valance*.

Possibly his most underrated film, *She Wore a Yellow Ribbon* should be singled out for its brilliant use of colour, deploying rich and muted hues to a sombre effect. In this transitional work, part of a trilogy (with *Fort Apache* (1948) and *Rio Grande* (1950)) about life in the United States cavalry, Ford praises the work of the military in settling the West, while diminishing the role of war in settling disputes.

The Searchers is now highly regarded by critics, historians, and such contemporary directors as Steven Spielberg, Martin Scorsese and George Lucas. It presents not only a rousing adventure tale, but also a sombre examination of the contradictions of settling the Old West. At the centre of the film Ethan Edwards (John Wayne) is portrayed as a bitter, ruthless and frustrated veteran of the Civil War who engages in an epic quest to retrieve his orphaned niece abducted by a Comanche raiding party.

This displaced man belongs neither to the civilised world of settlers clinging to the edge of Monument Valley nor to the proud but doomed Native Americans he doggedly pursues. Challenged and haunted by his respect for, but racist hatred of the Indians, Edwards speaks their language and is at home with their customs but is not deterred from seeking revenge for his murdered sister-in-law and her daughter.

In *The Searchers* Ford presents a brutal wilderness. There are no towns, only outposts and isolated homesteads. After years of searching, Ethan gently lifts his niece in his arms to take her home, back to a family which is long dead and to a homestead long deserted. It becomes a hollow and tragic heroic quest, but the Western myth persists above all (see Narrative & Form: Narrative theory).

Although Ford's final film was *Seven Women* (1966), *Cheyenne Autumn*, released in 1964 and his last film shot in Monument Valley, seems a more fitting close to a career begun some fifty years earlier. Ford made many of the most critically acclaimed films ever to come out of Hollywood, even as he managed to make a few of the worst. For further discussion of Fordian directorial status as auteur see Contexts: Cultural contexts.

narrative & form

narrative theory *p17*   **narrative deconstruction** *p20*

narrative theory

Making narratives, or stories, is a key way in which meanings are constructed in the media and outside them. Both factual and fictional forms are subject to this shaping.

Narrative theory suggests that stories in whatever media and whatever culture share certain features. This relates to the institutional context in which the text is produced.

Hollywood uses genre classification as a means to order narrative structure which is achieved by assigning codes and conventions to specific genres. Narrative theory studies the devices and conventions governing the organisation of a story (fictional or factual) into sequence. In order to examine the significance of the narrative structure of *Stagecoach*, it is important to examine appropriate theoretical approaches.

EQUILIBRIUM THEORY

Tzvetan Todorov, a Bulgarian structuralist linguist, published influential work on narrative from the 1960s onwards. Todorov argued that all stories begin with what he called an equilibrium.

Criticism of this theory has centred on its being based on a reworking of the cliché that every story has a beginning, a middle and an end. Its application to film narrative is still useful and can be found in a close textual reading. Todorov's equilibrium model not only deconstructs the narrative structure, but asks how the textual world is altered for 'better' or 'worse' in accordance with the impact of the final equilibrium being enforced.

MYTH AND GENRE

Alongside Todorov's structuralist approach the deployment of myth within the Western genre provides a meaningful examination of *Stagecoach*.

In the 1960s popular narratives (for example, established Hollywood genres such as the Western) began to be read via the structuralist approaches of Vladimir Propp.

Propp asserted that within popular cultural texts, the narratives contained the myth systems of contemporary societies. *Stagecoach* can be defined as a popular culture text, owing to its institutional context, generic structure, and popular audience reception.

The mythical status of the Western in relation to the nineteenth-century development of Northern America by European settlers is established within this genre on the basis of a white male sensibility. Ringo as hero can be fitted into this narrative structure through his status as mythical hero, something Wayne as a star has become, forever synonymous with the genre and inextricably linked to it (see Background: Key players' biographies, and see also Contexts: Character representation). Similarly, the mythical cowboy is perfectly aligned with the myth of the West and the environment (see Style: Set design and setting) which reflect 'his values' (see Contexts: Character representation). The hero also pursues a quest which must be achieved throughout the narrative course. The quest, however disrupted by such factors as the revenge structure which we see at work in *Stagecoach*, ultimately achieves the resolution in which the hero's position is reasserted by narrative closure.

THE NARRATIVE ROLE OF THE PICARESQUE

The text's narrative can be read as a picaresque adventure. The picaresque form is linked to literary and theatrical conventions in which wider issues relating to humanity can be considered by assembling a number of individuals, often diverse as is the case in *Stagecoach*, who share a journey. The adventures which befall these characters enable human nature to be examined.

The publicity still for *Stagecoach* which
shows star top billing for Claire Trevor

The publicity still which promotes *Stagecoach* highlights the importance of the picaresque to the narrative in promotion. The tag-lines 'The strangest adventure in frontier history!' and 'A wild ride packed with thrills!' both emphasise the picaresque element, playing down the human interest to be found in the diversity of character among the travellers, especially the binary opposition between the two women (see Contexts: Character representation) and what they represent in contrast to the strange collection of men who accompany them. The narrative progresses to reveal human 'goodness' and 'evil' as a result of events taking place inside the coach.

VIEWER'S UNDERSTANDING OF THE WESTERN GENRE

The narrative of *Stagecoach* is organised on the assumption that the viewer is familiar with the codes and conventions associated with the Western genre. It is assumed that the locations (see Style: Set design and setting), events (see Contexts: Genre) and characters (see Contexts: Character representation) are familiar.

The text is dubbed a 'classic' of the Western genre by critics. It is described as such because of its conventional narrative structure which subscribes to established generic codes and conventions, its use of location, its approach to law and order clearly marking the 'hero' and the 'villain', and its range of stock characters.

narrative deconstruction

By deconstructing the narrative events, the usefulness of Todorov's and Propp's assumptions, as well as of those of the viewer familiar with the Western genre, becomes evident.

The prologue can be interpreted as the opening equilibrium revealing that there is civil unrest caused by the Apache Indians near Lordsburg. Lordsburg is shown to be the final destination of the stagecoach. 'Apache warriors are on the warpath against white pioneers near the Arizona border with Mexico' (Tim Dirk, http://www.filmsite.orgistagec.html. Stagecoach Analysis, 1996).

The text immediately draws an ideological distinction between the Cheyenne Indians and the Apaches. This is indicated in the opening prologue, and also by casting a Cheyenne Indian as one of the couriers who reveal that the Apaches 'have burnt every building in sight'. The casting of the Apaches as textual evil 'other' is reflected in the white courier's assurance that the Cheyenne information is correct because the Cheyennes 'hate Apaches worse than we do'. It is assumed that the viewers know who the generic villains are. Although the Cheyenne report is trusted by white protagonists, it is significant that Ford does not confer 'equal' respect status on the former. This is indicated in the film grammar in which by lighting a character from below, the Indian's face assumes an 'evil' menacing quality contrasting with the 'clear' openly lit features of the white cavalry (see Contexts: Character representation).

The prologue serves the important narrative function of isolating the stagecoach party from the technological advances of communication. Arguably, the coach and the narrative would never be set in motion if the telegraph communication was not cut and the ambiguous yet prophetic word 'Geronimo' was interpreted. Structurally, the prologue serves to provide essential plot information and ideologically position the viewer.

The town of Tonto introduces the key characters (see Contexts: Character representation) and literally separates the occupants of the stagecoach from their 'civilised environment'. Tim Dirk (see above, p. 20) refers to this narrative section as a 'twelve minute expository sequence'. This is an apt summary and indicative of the time Ford allows to establish effectively the key members of the party. The time taken to introduce credible characters partly accounts for the text's success as the audience comes to care about the fate of some party members, and possess a point of view about the others.

'First leg of the trip': This narrative section is the key for establishing 'on the road conventions', notably the two-shot comical conversations between Curley and Buck, the stagecoach drivers. This feature is repeated whenever the text chooses to listen to Curley's and Buck's accounts. Most significantly this section introduces Wayne both in his film debut to the viewer, and to the other stagecoach passengers.

Ringo introduced

Wayne is introduced as seen from the moving stagecoach which associates Ringo with fluidity and action. The large clear close-up of Ringo's face is notable because it introduces the hero. This was important commercially as Wayne was still unknown to audiences at this point. His status as man of action is emphasised by Ringo's revolving and recocking his rifle and by his cry for the coach to 'Hold it!'

The dialogue serves a dual function of firstly breaking the equilibrium of the prologue owing to the late introduction of the key character. Secondly it denotes the changed events which are set into motion as a result of who Ringo is, and the implications of his impromptu joining the travelling party.

Even when not on horseback, Ringo is depicted at ease within the natural environment. This narrative treatment links with Propp's view that here the West and the individual hero are mythical symbols, as evidenced by the care which Ford takes to introduce him in this way.

The hero is linked to the strength and magnificence of the Western landscape which functions as his backdrop. Similarly, the earlier generic assumptions made about the viewer regarding the Indians as 'villains' are mirrored in Ringo being presented as a 'heroic' counterpart.

Dry Fork Way Station; the meal: The narrative events, notably the meal, are dealt with in detail in Contexts, as a suspension of the main narrative and an exposé of social norms and values.

'The Apache Wells (Mexican) outpost': The Apache woman Yakima is introduced in this narrative section although only defined in relation to her husband, Chris, and her status further diminished by Chris when he refers to her as 'my squaw' and a 'savage'. Although she has a name, it is mentioned only fleetingly in the narrative.

Chris's later response to his wife's flight reflects the text's equation of women with property (see Contexts: Character representation). Chris's quip, intended to raise a chuckle from the viewers, is revealing in this respect: 'I can find another wife, easy, yes, but not a horse like that.' This corroborates Edward Buscombe's view that 'Ford was always more indulgent towards sexism than racism' (*Stagecoach*, p. 54).

Two key events of the plot occur in this phase of the narrative. Doc redeems himself professionally and delivers Lucy Mallory's baby. Ringo and

Dallas recognise the depth of their romantic feelings for one another. Ringo faces a personal challenge, namely whether he should abscond, becoming a fugitive on the run, or stay and fulfil his promise of revenge. These events are analysed in depth later (see Contexts: Character representation). On discovering the Indian threat, Ringo decides to stay with the party.

'Final leg of the trip': This sees the party resume their travels, and the 'faceless others' (see Contexts: Character representation) become somewhat defined. The action sequence is made all the more exciting because the characters believe that they are out of danger and near to Lordsburg.

The eight-minute sequence (see Style: Special effects) focuses on one of the most ambitious action sequences ever recorded on celluloid.

The unexpected shooting of Buck creates a further crisis situation in which Ringo saves the passengers by straddling two panicking horses and steering them back. The rising tension which results in Hatfield's death is internally juxtaposed with the breakneck speed of exterior action.

Ford's criticism of Hatfield's effete Southern gentility inside the coach is starkly contrasted with Ringo's proactive action outside (see Contexts: Character representation).

Ringo's actions demonstrate the cowboy's ability in Fordian terms to shape nature (see Contexts: Character representation), forcing the horses to submit to his will and averting danger by his easy relationship with the natural environment.

The music associated with the cavalry charge and the bugle sound signify that due to Ringo's bravery the party are safe. As the travellers realise that they are safe, Hatfield speaks his dying words, ambiguously left unfinished: 'If you see Judge Greenfield, tell him his son ...'. Mystery surrounds Hatfield in death as it had in life; notably by the use of ominous close-ups in the carriage which suggest a 'shifty disposition' with something to hide. The fact that his father is a respected Southern judge had been a secret until his death. This is perhaps a further Fordian indictment of the Southern judicial system which in Hatfield's representation is 'at odds' with natural law (see Contexts: Cultural contexts).

'The town of Lordsburg': After the safe arrival in Lordsburg, social realignment takes place structurally. This is evidenced by the injured passengers departing from the coach escorted by the cavalry. Mrs Mallory first asks after her husband, his welfare unknown once the coach moved away from the bounds of 'civilisation'.

Assured that he is safe, Mrs Mallory attempts to thank Dallas for her selfless actions as a surrogate mother.

Existing textual readings and the dialogue indicate an attempt by Mrs Mallory to bridge the social chasm which has divided the women throughout the journey. There is an obvious link here with the discussion of Hollywood's deployment of binary oppositions in texts (see Contexts: Character representation). Women are weaker if they keep to the social structures that divide them. These two women share few looks and few words because they are unable to relate to each other socially. Dallas possesses the ability to see beyond social barriers, but owing to Mrs Mallory's conditioning her kindness falls on deaf ears.

Lucy's attempt to thank Dallas seems tokenistic and devoid of genuine compassion. Her words 'If there's ever anything I can do for ...' and Dallas's reply of 'I know' save Lucy from having to offer to Dallas open friendship in the 'civilised world'. One can speculate that the realist which Dallas has shown herself to be is patently aware that Lucy is incapable of extending friendship to her after their return to their prescribed social roles.

Mrs Mallory's actions contrast sharply with Mr Peacock who is in a similar physical condition, stretcher bound, but openly invites Dallas to Kansas. Ringo, meanwhile, talks to Curley and in his role of male protector offers his ranch and economic security to Dallas. He recognises that Dallas does not fit into Lordsburg: 'This is no town for a girl like her', a telling criticism of Lordsburg's norms and values.

Meanwhile, Gatewood meets his just punishment when the Sheriff fixes handcuffs not on Ringo as expected owing to his outlaw status, but on Gatewood who is guilty of a 'white collar' crime. The revelation that the telegraph wires have been repaired links with the fact that the purpose of Gatewood's journey has been to abscond with funds from Tonto to Lordsburg.

The final equilibrium is established here also for Ringo and Dallas, although significantly it is not a simple case of reaching the town. Dallas's 'shame' is witnessed by Ringo following her to the brothel which is hinted at as a sinful place. Ringo's persistence in declaring his love and 'honourable intentions' to Dallas is crosscut with the Plummer brothers Ike and Hank who join Luke Plummer in the saloon.

The crosscutting serves to remind the viewer that Ringo has not yet fulfilled his mythical revenge quest through which he can achieve true heroic status and reinstate the final equilibrium by avenging his family's death.

Ringo proposes marriage to Dallas who, drinking at the last chance marital saloon from a female perspective (see Contexts: Character representation), reacts with tearful gratitude: 'I'll never forget you asked me, Kid. That's somethin''.

Doc Boone in his 'guardian angel' role (see Contexts: Character representation) attempts to divert Luke from pursuing Ringo and to prevent further bloodshed.

The text works deftly from this point to conclude the revenge subplot. As Dirk observes (see Tim Dirk, http://www.filmsite.orgistagec.html. Stagecoach Analysis, 1996), the 'shootout scene, one of the shortest, most abbreviated shootouts in any Western on record' (see Contexts: Industrial), moves towards Ringo. The viewer is deceived, although it is questionable to what extent anyone believes that Wayne as the Kid will not triumph.

Viewer deception and the development of suspense are further evidenced by the copywriters setting the next morning's headline of: 'The Ringo Kid was killed on Main Street in Lordsburg tonight, and among the additional dead were ...'. True to generic form, the streets are cleared of all but the duellists. This in itself is an interesting stylistic and thematic concern of the Western in terms of 'civilised behaviour'. Shootouts of this nature occur in the town setting either within the saloon or on the streets directly outside it. The agency of law and order is suspended in favour of cowboy law in which somehow the 'naturally good' will triumph.

Dallas outside the brothel hears the shots, and her actions reveal the depth of her feelings, now fully defined in relation to the fate of her man, 'Ringo, Ringo, Ringo!' Her fear of his death is supported by the image of Luke Plummer and the absence of Ringo suggesting that in the bloody shootout Plummer is the victor. Plummer's fall is contrasted with Ringo's symbolic rise from the ashes, in this instance out of the shadows into the light, to be embraced by the ecstatic Dallas.

Ringo demonstrates his decency in his willingness, now that his heroic narrative quest is accomplished, to surrender to the forces of the law. Curley and Doc dispense their own brand of justice as Ringo and Dallas are whisked away by carriage to their ranch over the border. The ride into the sunset is literally a concluding image for the viewer.

The end equilibrium mirrors elements of the positive opening, notably when the major strain of *I Dream of Jeannie with the Light Brown Hair* is heard again (see Style: Sound effects – Musical score). The dramatic change in the opening credits to the minor key indicating the dangers of human nature and the Apache Indians, is absent at the end of the film as the danger is over, and Ford reestablishes Ringo's and Dallas's predestined 'natural' social order.

style

set design and setting *p27*   **costume and make-up** *p30*

lighting *p30*   **cinematography** *p31*   **colour/black and white** *p32*

special effects *p32*   **sound effects: musical score** *p33*

textual ownership and textual remakes *p39*

Mise-en-scène is an important tool of film analysis. *Stagecoach* creates meaning for a viewer through visual and auditory means. In addition to analysing the on-screen exchanges between characters, it is important to consider how they are informed by the visual aspects of the scene. The following categories provide a pertinent checklist not only for *Stagecoach* but also for Western genre indicators.

set design & setting

EXTERIOR INFORMING THEMATIC CONTENT

The film features Ford's favourite setting, Monument Valley, which has become synonymous with the director and genre as a result of this text's success (see Background: Director as auteur).

The film's form and mise-en-scène centring on Monument Valley (see Contexts: Filmography – Intertextual motifs) symbolically mediate thematic issues to a viewer. The smallness and potential frailty of the humans are contrasted with the age-old, vast natural landscape. Ford's reverence for Monument Valley is shown by the striking shots of Ringo against this background, actively changing narrative events by his heroic actions. The sheer size of Monument Valley, which is 5000 feet above sea level, emphasises the challenge of the travellers' journey.

The terrain is presented to a viewer as vast and dangerous, subject to unpredictable temperature extremes. The snow which held up the coach is not only metereologically accurate for the area, but serves as a religious symbol as well (see Contexts: Filmography – Intertextual motifs).

The location in *Stagecoach* is therefore of greater significance than simply providing an authentic setting. It possesses a spiritual quality, owing to its

landscape as a symbol

age and associations, reflected by Ringo's feeling 'at home' within its environs in contrast to the 'civilised' Lordsburg.

The landscape of the West is contrasted with the travelling stagecoach. The framing of the still (opposite) demonstrates how Ford makes scenic celluloid references to comment on a utopian existence. It epitomises Ringo's aim of realising a personal utopia, namely of a good man making his own mark on the landscape through a ranch community which complements nature, rather than through an eyesore which the sinful urban conurbations represent.

The endless sky which Ford achieves via a long shot emphasises the frailty of the people inside the stagecoach. The foregrounded natural flora and fauna emphasise that this is uncharted territory, and the striking view of the peaked mountains has a mystical quality. Ford's loving depiction of Monument Valley and the nineteenth-century West as he sees it romanticises a historical American period.

It is notable that the period is being recreated retrospectively and from a 1939 viewpoint. Cinema was being highly institutionalised during 1939; the medium was itself only forty-two years old, and Hollywood was establishing itself as an institutional context. Viewers would be encouraged to revel in the greatness of America at this period depicted in a still of this nature, particularly since the nation was attempting to regain its self-respect after the Great Depression.

THE TOWN

Tonto and Lordsburg were filmed in studio lots which aesthetically set 'civilisation' apart from the 'natural favoured' Monument Valley.

It is important to recognise that the choice of Lordsburg as end destination is ironic. The resolution of the narrative takes place there, but it exposes 'civilisation' as an immoral sham. This is shown by the revelation of Hatfield's true identity, by the loss of feminine solidarity between Lucy and Dallas when they are reassigned to their respective 'social categories', and by the exposure of Gatewood's 'white collar' corruption.

Buildings also suggest moral corruption, notably the saloon frequented by the Plummers and the bordello which appears to be Dallas's destination.

The vastness of Monument
Valley which stresses the frailty
of the stagecoach

The town's name, therefore, is linked to a wider textual theme, that appearances, including socially assigned names, can be deceptive and true goodness cannot be manufactured (see Lighting).

costume & make-up

The style of *Stagecoach* reaped commercial dividends outside the world of the film owing to the 'look' of the leading lady, Claire Trevor. Claire Trevor served an additional promotional function in sporting a contemporary 'take' on a hairstyle which was based on elements associated with the historical setting of the film, as detailed in a promotional poster, 'While Miss America is dashing to the smartest shops and the swankiest hairdressers to have her shapely self draped with the very latest in clothing and to have her hair "upswept", she is actually purchasing 1885 styles.'

lighting

The text's lighting anticipates Hollywood's characteristic 1940s style. Typically it uses low key lighting effects, including chiaroscuro and the use of strong shadows. These techniques are usually associated with the film noir movement which stylistically emphasises themes of urban corruption, 'deadly' women, crime, and features mysterious plots and subplots. Examples of film noir include *Double Indemnity* (1944), and the movement is seen as starting with *The Maltese Falcon* in 1941.

Ford's stylistic choices confirm his status as an auteur as he favours those which are usually regarded as outside established Western trends. The text does not subscribe to studio-defined genre production components.

Stagecoach is a hybrid inasmuch as Ford draws on other generic elements such as melodrama to present a bleaker picture of humanity and to challenge contemporary social values. The last sequence in Lordsburg which operates as a dénouement makes continued use of low key lighting. A possible explanation for this may be that Lordsburg is exposed as a 'civilised' town which offers less than its religious name promises.

lighting conveys a message

This Western 'holy land' is filled with saloons and brothels, frequented by the Plummer brothers, and offers revelations of Gatewood's corruption. The use of low key lighting emphasises these undesirable urban elements which contrast with the well-lit 'wilderness' sequences in Monument Valley. The narrative resolution further emphasises this in Ringo's and Dallas's departure from Babylon for the preferable Western country of Ringo's ranch.

cinematography

Closely linked to lighting, the cinematography of *Stagecoach* also presents 'civilisation' negatively in contrast to the utopian vision of Monument Valley. Ford makes use of artificial studio based lighting techniques to emphasise the danger facing the protagonists and to comment on the environment. The tone achieved by using Monument Valley and natural light allows nature to speak for itself and be seen as a preferable 'pure' alternative to the man-made capitalist America which is coming into being in the expanding towns of Tonto and Lordsburg.

FOCUS

The use of deep focus is pioneered in *Stagecoach* alongside unconventional lighting techniques atypical for the genre. This is further validation of Ford's auteur status, because he imposes his own stylistic choices on the genre to clarify the meaning. An example of this is given in the Lighting section above, showing how low key lighting directs the viewer how to decode Lordsburg in contrast to Monument Valley.

In *Stagecoach* (p. 58) Edward Buscombe refers to a comment by Orson Welles comparing the innovative use of film grammar in *Stagecoach*. Welles possesses an auteur status and a reputation for exercising his own brand of film grammar. The use of deep focus in *Citizen Kane* (1941) has itself achieved legendary film analysis status. 'John Ford was my teacher. My own style has nothing to do with his, but Stagecoach was my movie text-book. I ran it over forty times.'

72942

colour/black & white

Owing to Walter Wanger's straitened economic position at United Artists the studios would not permit the extra budgetary expense involved in shooting and printing *Stagecoach* in colour. In the mid 1930s 30% was added to production costs as a result of printing a colour film.

Despite the enforced use of monochrome film stock, stylistically *Stagecoach* benefits from the chiaroscuro deployed in the low key lighting sequences discussed above. Chiaroscuro heightens the distinctions between light and darkness in a frame. It also links to textual issues thematically: characters who are regarded as 'socially' good, notably Gatewood, Hatfield and Mrs Mallory, are shown by the use of lighting to be inferior to the 'innate goodness' of Ringo, Doc and Dallas. Stylistic features are therefore operating in tandem with content, and a viewer is creating meaning by reading the visual elements of a film frame rather than simply relying on direct plot and character based action.

special effects

Enos Yakima Canutt performs most of the incredible stunts in the film. Ford did permit Wayne to carry out most of his own stunts, including the jumping from horse to horse when the coach is about to go out of control. Canutt roomed with Wayne in a small cabin during the on-location shooting, teaching him stunts.

Commercially this daring debut confirmed Wayne's success as an action hero. The attack on the stagecoach was made by more than three hundred Navajo Indians from the Arizona reservation, who, like the stagecoach, averaged forty-six miles per hour on horseback across the flat plains of Monument Valley.

The notorious live stunt featured in the climactic eight-minute action sequence, involves an Apache Indian (Canutt) leaping from his horse in a bid to grab the reins of the leading horse, thus literally seizing control. The Apache is shot and falls under the thundering hooves. The realistic aesthetic achieved in this sequence is manifested by the injured Apache rising to his knees, which would not have been possible if a stage dummy had been used, as might have been expected at this production phase of Hollywood's history.

sound effects: musical score

A multitude of composers including John Leipold, Leo Shuken, Gerard Carbonara, W. Franke Harling and Richard Hageman are credited as contributors to the text's score. Shared musicianship was an essential requirement owing to the demands of a speedy release schedule. Carbonara's name does not appear in the screen credits, but Louis Gruenberg's does even though his music was not used. The 1939 Oscar for Best Score went to all except these last two.

Hageman's skill centred on interlacing recognised American folk songs, themselves musical myths linking with the application of Proppian theory to the text (see Narrative & Form: Narrative theory). Ford formed a musical partnership with Hageman on six subsequent texts which further contributed to Ford's auteur status. By working with a composer selected by himself, Ford was responsible for creative control, and although keeping within studio established practices and genres, the text is imprinted with an individual directorial vision.

Stagecoach won Best Score award for its compilation of seventeen American folk tunes of the 1880s. Music is a significant textual indicator within *Stagecoach* and tells the viewer how to decode the text.

The opening credits present the viewer with the main title, and patriotic music in a major key introduces the white protagonists. The upbeat tempo engages a viewer as it suggests action and excitement, both common elements within the Western genre.

On introduction of the Apache Indians, however, the music distinctly adopts a minor key which presents connotations of threat and a harsh discord hinting at a hostile presence.

Associative musical motifs are a further means to organise the viewer's reading of social group representation ideologically. This is supported by

music as a backdrop

the track listing references which in their titles indicate the key moments in the narrative. The total time of the track listing is 45:23 and the lengthy duration of music is indicative of how music can function within film form and structure to create an appropriate atmosphere.

The non diegetic use of music throughout the text suggests that its function is to act as a backdrop to visual sequences which Ford references by continual contrasts between the inside of the coach, which is at times stultifying and unbearable, and the landscape outside. The passengers appear in the film frame composition to be alternatively trapped and shunned (Dallas and Ringo in particular). This is contrasted with the outside environment (see Set design and setting) glimpsed by the viewer; and further revealed in the showdown between the Apaches and Ringo. For the visual driven aspects of the narrative when Ford presents tableaux of the outside world, the reaction shots of the protagonists which reveal their 'true' dispositions, and the action battle sequence music form a key textual element.

An analysis of the track's titles and narrative function is useful here to demonstrate the significance of music in the film:

Main title: The genre setting function is achieved by the integration of *I Dream of Jeannie with the Light Brown Hair*. The 'heroic' cowboy's major key is contrasted with the minor key forces of the enemy Apache Indians. In conjunction with the music the opening credits set in Playbill typeface also function as associative iconography. The Playbill font favoured by Ford was by the time the film was released a favoured Western choice, and by the use of an established credit typeface audiences are immediately made aware what genre of film they are about to see.

Dryfork saloon/ Stagecoach arrives (1:14): This sets the scene for the introduction of the key characters and the stagecoach collection point. The music functions as sound support for the movement of the characters, notably Doc and Dallas who must walk past members of the disapproving 'civilised' community. Setting the sparse dialogue to music reinforces the viewer's impression about the function of the characters and the text's social perceptions of 'good and 'bad' characters (see Narrative & Form: Narrative deconstruction).

sound effects

It is important to recognise that Ford is not an uncritical proponent of the American ideology advocated by the pious Law and Order brigade, as he uses a range of celluloid devices, notably the 'star' positions of the actors playing Doc and Dallas, as an institutional context to inform the viewer that these characters' actions are ideologically preferable. Previous positive associations with the names of Thomas Mitchell and Claire Trevor are sufficient visual indicators to cast them as 'good' from a viewer's perceptions (see Background: Key players' biographies, and Contexts: Production history).

This is starkly contrasted with the negative treatment of the Law & Order League women in this sequence. Ford achieves this by deploying celluloid devices and assembling a performance tableau, as shown in the discussion of the still overleaf.

This still is an excellent example of how a character's status can be mediated via the reaction shots of other protagonists. The clearly identified Law & Order League women are presented as being horror stricken, humorously not by the later 'real' threat of the Apache Indians but by characters who are granted heroic status in the film.

The group of women with varying facial expressions of disapproval is placed between Doc's and Dallas's introduction informing the viewer via this visual insert about the moral attitudes of society. The unflattering depiction of these women by Ford, notably the sharp focus framing which emphasises the etched lines of disgust on the women's faces, is sharply contrasted with the diffused light cast on Dallas.

Film grammar therefore is working on Dallas's behalf to subtly inform the viewer that visually she is more attractive, and the 'evil' presence is visually suggested by the grouping of four hag-like women. The women's pose with arms tightly folded suggesting disapproval, coupled with the varying heights of the women huddled in a tableau, works collectively to suggest that they represent a restrictive industrialised society and a hypocritical legal system. The shadow on the face of the third woman from the left also serves to align the women with darkness when contrasted with the brightness and soft lighting associated with Dallas. This analysis is intended to demonstrate that visual composition of shots and the

a hag-like grouping

The women of the Law & Order
League presented deliberately
in an unflattering sharp focus
to underline their uncharitableness

juxtaposition achieved by editing form a speedy device to direct the viewer's opinions on the characters.

A new passenger (1:44): This introduces John Wayne to the characters and the viewers simultaneously. The figure of Ringo standing out against the Fordian landscape is an iconographic feature of Ford's texts and a code and convention of the Western genre itself (see Background: Key players' biographies, and Contexts: Genre). Wayne's entrance is supported by a musical motif which ruptures the text's equilibrium as Ringo is a social outcast and associated with violence.

Family history (4:35): This lengthy section of musical score is an important support scene setter in revealing plot and character information. Ringo is granted heroic status in this sequence as he forms a romantic alliance with Dallas and reveals the rationale behind his violent acts (see Contexts: Character representation).

First Born (1:34): This sequence of music has relevance to Mrs Mallory giving birth to her first child and the importance of an innocent child being introduced into the narrative. The howl of the coyote which welcomes the baby into American society, is an interesting auditory and visual image to deploy because it is associated with nature rather than 'civilisation'.

Outside Yakima sings a Spanish song which is an exile's lament for the native land and a love song to the Mexican stagepost hands. This has relevance to the position of social outcasts in which Ringo and Dallas find themselves, and to the increasingly romantic nature of their relationship (see Contexts: Character representation).

All is forgiven (2:37): The forgiveness can be seen as extended to Doc, Dallas and Ringo. Ringo is torn between escaping from the stagecoach team or staying with the party.

Escape route (1:53): This refers to the narrative climax in which Ringo must decide whether to escape or remain with the party. It is significant that it further refers to the attempts of the stagecoach to chart an escape route from the Apaches. The initial reaction of the party is to escape rather than face the Apache threat and attack. This musical sequence lends itself to the accelerated narrative pace and external sequences in which the viewer is following an action-driven sequence with brief snatches of informative dialogue.

No more Indians (1:08): This track includes the notorious stunt performed in the film, and the recognition of Ringo as an action hero (see Special effects). Contrasting with the stagecoach occupants, the track underscores Wayne's individualism as he pits himself against the wild horses which pose a threat alongside the Apache Indians whom he destroys (see Contexts: Ideology).

Cheyenne saloon (0:35): On reaching Lordsburg this small sequence offers euphemistic sound support to the oblique visual revelation to the viewer and to Ringo of Dallas's prostitute status. Owing to the Hays Production Code issues of sexuality were not permitted to be directly represented and film grammar has to work around the ban by presenting a visual tableau.

Get out of town (2:41): This is an aptly named track which concludes Ringo's quest for revenge for the murder of his family. The track title is inextricably linked to the 'cowboy' function of riding into town and driving out the evil presence. The shootout is effectively underscored by the music which directs the viewer's perception of the characters' status and actions. Ringo's ability to despatch swiftly the Western enemy in much the same way as he had despatched the Apache Indians validates his commanding status in the narrative.

Stagecoach to Cheyenne (1:24): This song which closes the narrative, supports the resolution in which the viewer sees Ringo's and Dallas's departure from a community which despite their 'natural goodness' is unable to accommodate them (see Contexts: Character representation). The music links to Doc's final remark that their departure to Ringo's ranch is preferable to living in the fast expanding industrial world. The complimentary musical tempo to dialogue leaves the viewer with a satisfactorily restored equilibrium in which the hero rides off into the sunset and 'gets the girl'.

SPECIAL EFFECTS AND FORDIAN FILM GRAMMAR

The following quotation from Buscombe's *Stagecoach* (p. 64), refers to the action sequence lasting eight minutes forty-eight seconds: 'In that time there are 104 shots, giving an average shot length of five seconds. According to Tag Gallagher, the average shot length of the rest of the film is 10.5 seconds. But it's not the sheer speed of the cutting that creates the excitement. The whole film has been building to this moment, constantly postponed yet always foreseen. Ford demonstrates his individualistic approach to film grammar and frame composition in this action sequence which allows him to reject one of the cardinal rules of the classical era of Hollywood cinema, the so-called 180-degree system (see Cinematography).

textual ownership & textual remakes

The question of textual ownership surrounds *Stagecoach*. The argument centres on the backer, Walter Wanger, who later claimed that the text was his own idea and that Ford was little more than a contract director. Such claims extended to the value of John Wayne as a star commodity: Wanger claimed he had discovered Wayne in B movies.

Wanger's claims were vehemently denied by Ford who issued statements asserting his individual status in creatively conceiving the text and casting Wayne. Wanger later distanced himself from his earlier claims about creative control.

Stagecoach was successfully reissued many times, and usually billed alongside *Long Voyage Home* (1940). Over the years, its original negative prints were either destroyed or lost, but fortunately Wayne provided his personal copy of the film for reproduction and preservation in 1970.

In 1966, *Stagecoach* was remade starring Alex Cord and Ann-Margret in leading roles with Bing Crosby cast in the role of the drunken doctor. It was a commercial and critical failure, validating the largely held view that the original text resisted remake and should be critically revered rather than commercially imitated.

The original *Stagecoach* film was released in 1939, a stellar year for Westerns, with such blockbusters as *Destry Rides Again* and *Jesse James* in

ownership & remakes

cult status of *Stagecoach*

the lists, but it was *Stagecoach* that captured all the plaudits, and rightly so, with Ford winning the New York Critics' Award for his spectacular film. Footage from this film classic surfaced in some B movies later, notably in *I Killed Geronimo* (1950) and *Laramie Mountains* (1952). The text acquired a renewed cult status as a result.

contexts

ideology *p41*　　**character representation** *p42*

cultural contexts *p62*　　**filmography: intertextual motifs** *p65*

genre *p67*　　**production history** *p68*　　**industrial** *p70*　　**audience** *p72*

ideology

TEXTUAL IDEOLOGICAL ORIENTATION

The text demonstrates how Hollywood can operate as an ideological state apparatus in its role as a mass media agent. From the raising of the American flag as a symbol of 'goodness' and 'white man's civilised rule', the viewer is aware of the importance of protecting the American land which is being gradually 'civilised'. Civilisation is textually defined by the growing city communities which are being fashioned by white settlers (see Style: Set design and setting).

It is significant to note to whom this American protection is granted. The ideological 'others' are defined as the Apache Indians who remain the 'faceless enemy' for the greater part of the text until the final battle which results in a violent assertion of white male authority. This is a common trend within the narrative of the Western, building up suspense and establishing 'white supremacy' by positioning the viewer so as to relate to the main protagonists. Their faces and characteristics have been systematically developed for the viewer in the course of the narrative, which encourages a preferred reading of identification with the heroic cowboys who are upholding and safeguarding the burgeoning American civilisation.

In this instance, it is the white occupants of the stagecoach who are not granted 'equal' textual status in terms of 'goodness' and how a viewer should respond to them. The fact that the travellers belong to different social classes is symbolic and it is noteworthy that not all of the party survive. All of them, however, are initially protected by the American flag by being able to travel together in this fashion.

character representation

JOHN WAYNE: 'THE RINGO KID'

The effects of the star system are evident to a viewer in the opening credits which bill Claire Trevor above John Wayne (see Production history). Ordinarily the male star is given precedence over his female counterpart reflecting the patriarchal institutional context to which Hollywood subscribes. The billing reflects Wayne's debut Hollywood status at the production time. The publicity still featuring both Trevor and Wayne exemplifies how Wayne has been introduced in relation to Trevor's existing star status in Hollywood (see Background: Key players' biographies).

The foregrounding focus on Trevor indicates how Wayne is defined in relation to her. The romantic relationship which develops in the narrative is implied by the happy faces of both of them, and is emphasised by the choice of a close head shot which underlines their feelings. In addition, the touching headshots imply a romantic relationship. Wayne is therefore established not only as an individual, as discussed in the publicity shot for Ringo (see p. 44), but as a leading man capable of wooing the leading lady.

This makes Wayne and the cowboy hero more bankable as a result, as a love story dimension within any genre increases its appeal to the mass audience. Arguably, the action sequences appeal to the male contingent whilst the focal female character Dallas and the romantic subplot appeal to the female viewer (see Style: Costume and make-up).

Wayne's debut is particularly significant because it establishes his star persona as an archetypal cowboy. The belief system which he expounds textually becomes the main ideological element of the Western (see Genre).

Similarly, the genre and the star are imbued with a renewed signifier. The 'kid' status conferred on Ringo links with Wayne's star status in Hollywood. In his star infancy, when this motion picture was produced, it provided an opportunity for Wayne to establish himself. On seeing or hearing his

In the publicity still of Wayne
and Trevor the lighting foregrounds
Trevor as the star of the film

John Wayne as Ringo,
establishing in this debut
his cowboy image

name in connection with Western texts the viewer knows at once what to expect from Wayne's character which is defined by his actions in *Stagecoach*.

The publicity still of Wayne demonstrates how his debut established the persona of John Wayne, 'the Duke', the archetypal cowboy. Costume is symbolically significant, and it is notable that it still hints at Ringo's position as a loner. The backdrop of the natural environment, albeit a studio shot, epitomises Ringo's affinity with the natural Western environment rather than with self-imposed social laws. The casual angle of his hat contrasts sharply with Hatfield's and Gatewood's 'respectfully' worn hats, following fashion rather than the carefree practical style which Ringo adopts.

The trademark kerchief and denims make Ringo's appearance functional and appropriate for the practical activities which he pursues. Jane Gaines has described Wayne's shirt as having 'a kind of fortified or armoured look, reinforcing the authoritarian aura of the mature Wayne person' (E. Buscombe (ed.), *BFI Companion to the Western*, entry on 'Costume', p. 100). His appearance also validates his masculine strength within the text conferring an unconventional soldier status upon him.

The freshfaced open stance which Wayne adopts for this still promotes viewer identification as the 'kid' character tag neatly tallies with Wayne's debut performance. The bright-eyed slightly smiling face matches the open body language. This links with Ringo's persona; a straight-talking cowboy who takes people as he finds them and makes no secret about his duty to avenge the killing of his family.

Wayne is presented as a maverick protagonist, governed by the rules of the natural environment (see Style: Set design and setting). He upholds the law of white men, but on his own terms, not according to the constricting 'civilised' laws. The fact that Wayne is called 'the Ringo kid' gives him a notoriety which is absent when his Christian name, Henry, is used.

Ringo is not a member of the initial stagecoach party which makes his later introduction enigmatic and adds a dimension of excitement for the viewer because of his apparent unknowable status. Questions abound about the motives for his revenge, and his dangerous reputation establishes Wayne as a strong archetypal male protagonist (see Narrative & Form: Narrative deconstruction).

Ringo responds warmly to Doc and Dallas, seeing himself as another outcast who is judged on the crimes he has committed, without regard to the rationale behind his thirst for revenge.

DOC JOSIAH BOONE

The role of Doc is instrumental in offering the viewers a sympathetic point of view towards Ringo and Dallas. Doc is introduced in his 'natural environment', namely a saloon bar, desperately trying to convince the barman to let him have a drink 'on the tab'. Doc's voice increasingly gains narrative credibility, and the viewer is encouraged to give it weight as events progress.

Doc Boone acts as the voice of reason in the film, which is all the more acceptable ideologically because of his human imperfections. His weakness for drink enables a viewer to gain a human insight into decent Christian values which oppose the constricting value judgements made by the Law & Order League women. Doc refers to them as 'dregs of the time' and his humorous wry observations instruct as well as entertain.

The studio publicity still depicting Thomas Mitchell as Doc demonstrates that in Fordian terms appearances can be deceptive. Morality is a central textual thematic concern, evidenced by the duplicity of Hatfield and Gatewood, the so-called 'decent gentlemen' (see Character representation, Hatfield and Gatewood, below).

Doc is a humorous iconoclast who is on the side of the youthful goodness of Ringo and Dallas. His appearance and star persona warrant discussion, as Mitchell received the ultimate Hollywood plaudits for this role: the Academy Award. The jaunty angle of his hat recalls Ringo's individualism, wearing his hat as a symbol of his character rather than following social dictates. The glance away from the camera and slightly jocular expression are indicative of Doc's enquiring mind and wisdom. The slightly hunched gesture with arms folded shows him at ease rather than enacting a social role.

The still of Thomas Mitchell
captures Doc Boone's character:
sardonic, amused, mocking the
conventions, faintly disreputable

His unshaven face is a direct flouting of convention, sporting the stubble of everyday life, and linking with his life as an alcoholic. It is also in direct contrast with the clean-shaven gentlemen in the carriage and with Hatfield's carefully tended moustache, which appears effete in comparison with Doc's rugged masculinity.

This observation is pertinent in the textual revelation of Hatfield's cowardice when faced with the threat of the Apache Indians. Doc's abbreviation of his professional title defies the constraints of the stereotypical doctor. It is shown to be textually telling as he is the 'bar room philosopher' who triumphs over the dangers of the hostile environment through which the stagecoach party must travel.

Mrs Mallory's confinement provides the opportunity for Doc to progress from drunken buffoon to professional doctor. His 'drying out' by consuming copious cups of coffee enables him to minister to Mrs Mallory.

His ironic toast of 'good health' in the coach when the journey is resumed serves to rupture the temporary peaceful equilibrium established by the baby's birth. The irony is underlined when Mr Peacock is shot by an arrow at this very moment. Doc's telling final comment closes the narrative and summarises Ford's psychological examination of a cross-section of humanity travelling together. When bidding farewell to Ringo and Dallas on the way to marriage and the ranch, Doc remarks, 'They're safe from the blessings of civilisation'. Viewers are encouraged to view Ringo's actions as preferable to the vagaries of the law which protects scoundrels like Hatfield and Gatewood.

HATFIELD

Hatfield is first shown gambling, a vice which is revealed to be symbolic of his textual positioning. He serves as a reminder to viewers that appearances can be deceptive and allows Ford to expose social notions of gentlemanly conduct.

This is achieved by granting him initial social respectability as a self-appointed protector of Mrs Mallory, supposedly his altruistic reason for joining the party. This is particularly ironic when considering his later actions when he almost kills her during the attack by Apache Indians.

oblique representation of violence

Hatfield covering a woman killed
by the Apaches, a portent of the
violence which the stagecoach
passengers are trying to escape

Hatfield operates as a foil to Ringo in the way he upholds certain social principles but proves himself to be uncharitable by his rude behaviour towards Dallas. Hatfield's deliberate snubbing of Dallas at the first meal stop serves to emphasise Ringo's inherent goodness as he shows up Hatfield's 'chivalrous' conduct by pointedly offering Dallas a seat.

The narrative crisis of the journey finds Gatewood and Hatfield arguing instead of uniting as a party to counteract the Apache Indian threat. Hatfield is about to commit the heinous self-revelatory act of killing Mrs Mallory when he himself is killed by an Apache arrow. His departure from the narrative is essential owing to his evil status, and becomes a textual ideological statement about what constitutes real gentlemanly conduct.

Hatfield's Southern origins are significant in relation to Ford's personal social polemic. The 'negative' representation of Hatfield is the antithesis of Western American values embodied by the Ringo Kid. It is critically supported within the generic framework by the negative treatment of Southern characters. The South's representative is Hatfield, the only one of the nine party members who fails to survive the journey into Western democracy.

GATEWOOD

Gatewood occupies a similar narrative position to Hatfield in that he is granted social respectability. The text reveals that his social position is dubious, from both an ethical and a legal standpoint. At the start of the journey the textual mystery of Gatewood receiving a message when the telegraph line has been out of order is a clue that he is perhaps not who he purports to be.

Ford criticises America's free market enterprise epitomised by the capitalist expansion of urbanised areas through Gatewood who declares that 'what this country needs is a business man for president' (see Background: Director as auteur).

Gatewood's harangue defines him in terms of money and a free enterprise individualism at the expense of respect and concern for his fellow human beings. Gatewood's cowardice which becomes evident when the Apache

Indians prove most threatening represents the opposite of Ringo's courageous resolve to face any threats that come his way.

Ford's examination of bravery casts Hatfield and Gatewood as cowardly 'gentlemen' who are likely, as Doc earlier remarks, to shoot someone in the back. They lack Ringo's dependable straightforward resolve. Gatewood creates more chaos for the party than the threat of the Apache Indians when he collapses into hysteria in the face of pressure.

Doc punches Gatewood and asserts himself physically, so adding to his continuous voice of Fordian reason. Gatewood is finally arrested in a befitting narrative resolution. It is significant that Ringo's act of natural justice allows him to shed his socially assigned criminal status, whilst Gatewood despite his gentlemanly status is revealed to be just a common criminal.

MR PEACOCK

In spite of his apparently unassuming narrative status Mr Peacock's character is significant in representing the decent qualities of the 'little man'. His profession as a whiskey drummer aligns him with Doc, and he asserts himself at significant narrative junctures.

He is given the 'little man' status because he is seen as insignificant by his fellow travellers. He makes his presence felt, however, after the birth of Mrs Mallory's baby when he puts to shame the behaviour of both Gatewood and Hatfield.

Peacock's survival after he has been shot by an arrow contrasts starkly with Hatfield's fate. Peacock is granted narrative survival because of his inherent goodness. This is reflected in his parting comment to Dallas when, in contrast to Mrs Mallory, he openly flouts social convention and invites Dallas to Kansas City. He is addressed by the other travellers as Hancock or Haycock, which is thought to be an intertextual reference to Ernest Haycox, author of the story on which the film is based.

Physically, Mr Peacock demonstrates the textual theme that appearances can be deceptive as his sober suit, timid body language and nondescript appearance lead to his being taken for a preacher rather than a whiskey drummer. It is revealed that he became a whiskey drummer as a result of his wife's inheritance, which suggests that she is a woman not to be disobeyed. This introduces a further humorous twist, suggesting perhaps that Peacock's masculinity and social identity are obscured by an unseen overpowering female presence.

THE APACHE INDIANS AS 'OTHER'

The most negative representation of a social group in the text is that of the Apache Indians who exist in the main as a faceless 'other'. This is reflected throughout the narrative as when the stagecoach party are warned by the military that they can be given no protection against the threat posed by the Apache Indians. The text partially mediates a human representation of the Apaches through Dallas when she speaks of the moralising white community as being worse than the threat of the Apaches.

The narrative resolution is driven towards white male supremacy, however, when Ringo repels the attacking Apaches single-handed. Doc, Ford's moral conscience within the film, condones the destruction of the Apache Indians through his comment about Geronimo as the 'old Apache butcher'. By the reference to Geronimo as an unseen (to the viewer) butcher the viewer is positioned to accept a preferred reading that the Apaches are the enemy and some members of the white travelling party are the heroes.

The still opposite is an excellent example of how the delineation between white character reaction shots and the representation of the Apache Indians as a faceless mass is achieved. The attempted retreat of the stagecoach is shown in the background. The foreground of the frame, however, shows the fall of an Apache Indian. Further Apache presence is blurred, with little definition of a particular character's face. The Apache Indians are also denied reaction shots, an important device in film for establishing a well-defined character and encouraging the viewer to identify with or learn about a character's intentions.

The reaction shots are mediated from the white occupants of the stagecoach showing their fear of what the Apache Indians may do to them if they are captured. The speed of film on which the action sequences are shot further supports the 'mass' presence of the Apache Indians.

The attacking Apache Indians,
though in the foreground, still
remain the faceless enemy against
the clear lines of the coach

Ford's own ideology

Ford in *Stagecoach* asserts his own dominant ideology, which is at odds with the corporate industrialisation of America which was taking place at the close of the nineteenth century (see Background: Director as auteur).

Favoured characters in a Ford text must posses some 'natural' goodness, which does not always coexist with social conventions. The textual analysis of Ringo, Dallas and Doc stresses this point. Ringo is the hero because he is aligned with the environment and naturally adapts to the challenges that it presents. The ingenuity he shows in taming the panicking horses and fighting the Apache Indians in a maverick style is a testimony to this. Interestingly, Ford presents the viewer with an action-filled sequence in which Ringo can destroy the collective threat of the Apache Indians, thus confirming his status as an archetypal Western hero.

This has become a convention of New Hollywood cinema, dominated by the action hero and his sensational exploits. Bruce Willis in the *Die Hard* series presents a variation on a Western hero. Scarred by the changes in his 'natural' environment and the threat to his family structure he seeks an impromptu revenge against an expanding corporate culture. Like Ringo, he achieves this on his own by pitting his physical strength against the challenges which the 'other' represents. He also is a victor using unconventional methods.

MRS MALLORY

Mrs Mallory is introduced at the opening of the narrative as a 'respectable woman', as indicated by her being married to the unseen Captain Mallory. Her name defines her at once in relation to her 'brave heroic husband' who is fighting the 'white man's cause', iconographically represented by the flying American flag discussed above (p. 41).

Mrs Mallory is in danger at the beginning of the narrative which is made all the more significant because she is a woman. She is travelling alone, which is potentially perilous as 'respectable women' should be under the protection of their husbands.

This links with the textual theme of duty. Duty to the white American cause is greater than duty to individual humans and supersedes the secondary important theme of family. Captain Mallory, engaged in carrying out his higher duty for his country, awaits his wife to join him so that the wider concern of 'American values' (another ideological link) can be combined with the arrival of his wife and soon to be born child.

Mrs Mallory's pregnancy makes the binary opposition in the textual reading all the more relevant. From a viewer's point of view, it is interesting that Mrs Mallory's pregnancy in itself is not made obvious until the second stop when she 'swoons' and an offscreen confinement takes place. This is important because it textually reflects the ideological censorship controls operating in Hollywood at this time, namely the Hays Production Code (see Industrial, below).

The sudden revelation of Mrs Mallory's condition is euphemistically suggested. The viewer must make earlier connections as to why there was undue male concern in the stagecoach about how she is feeling. Her stiff, voluminous garments (themselves reflective of how the female form is bound into a respectable social outer casing) hide her obvious pregnancy.

Arguably, a textual rationale for this is to subscribe to the legislative requirements of the Hays Production Code. If Mrs Mallory's pregnancy was obvious, it would be a continuous symbolic signifier that she was sexually active, permissibly because within the religious and legal bounds of marriage resulting in procreation. Mrs Mallory's binary opposition, however, functions as an impossible male ideal: the married woman who is presented as virginal (see Female representation and Hollywood, below). By not drawing undue attention to her pregnancy, Mrs Mallory's virginal appeal can be textually sustained and the binary opposition strengthened.

On boarding the stagecoach she is defined as a fragile, vulnerable innocent who should be given male protection. She is passed into the dubious safekeeping of Hatfield (see Character representation, Hatfield, above).

Unable to protect herself because of her female vulnerability, Mrs Mallory functions as an object to be protected. Her appearance is presented as angelic, reinforced by the film grammar which presents her face in soft, flattering diffused lighting and focus imparting an angelic glow. Her face appears luminous, an impression heightened by her bonnet, which draws away all hair from her face. This impression is supported by further references to Mrs Mallory as an 'angel'.

The stopovers (see Narrative & Form: Narrative deconstruction) are important because they allow the overall plot of the travellers' journey towards a final destination to be temporarily halted. The purpose of this is to enable the reader gradually to incline towards favouring specific characters by learning more about them. The stopovers are of particular value to a film and media studies student because they offer criticism of the institutional context and American social values.

In relation to Mrs Mallory's textual status, her respectability is recognised in the scene of the meal. This has symbolical significance because meals have a wider social function in revealing the manners and attitudes of the characters who represent a microcosm of America. Mrs Mallory's preferences are consulted at the expense of Dallas, and it is particularly significant that Mrs Mallory refuses to sit next to her. Visually this underscores the separation of binary types which operates between Mrs Mallory and Dallas.

The picaresque narrative strand resumes, and Mrs Mallory becomes unwell owing to her advanced pregnancy, still only vaguely hinted at rather than explicitly represented for the reasons discussed earlier. Dallas's offer of feminine comfort and solidarity to Mrs Mallory ('you can put your head on my shoulder') is rebuffed, once again indicating her 'social untouchability'.

DALLAS

Dallas is defined at the opening of the narrative in terms of her profession. As a prostitute she belongs to the 'sinful whore' category which defines the second female binary opposition.

Dallas's name is highly symbolic. Mrs Mallory's identity is defined exclusively in relation to her husband's, granting her her respectable social status. She is literally the property of a respectable man. Dallas's name, by contrast, hints at urbanisation. Urbanisation is traced in the narrative, notably in the physical battle between the 'white military' and 'Apache Indians' for land and property rights. The 'civilised settlements' which are growing to form urbanised modern America reflect a certain type of white male power (see Style: Set design and setting).

Dallas's initial appearance further serves to mark the differences between Mrs Mallory and herself. Her tighter-fitting fashionable garments serve to accentuate the sexuality of the female form. While Mrs Mallory's plain hairstyle brings into relief her angelic face, Dallas's fashionable curls, painted eyebrows and mouth highlight the contrast between the two women.

Hollywood has a longstanding tradition of equating cities with sinful pursuits, and both Dallas's name and profession suggest this. From Murnau's *Sunrise* in which a couple leave the protection of their natural environment to explore the 'sinful' city, this is still a prevalent concern for New Hollywood. Note that in *Seven* (1995) evil is running amok in the city setting and constant references are made to the 'good' protagonists' hate of the city. Such connotations are present in Dallas's name, which depersonalises her because she is assigned an urbanised identity devoid of individuality.

Dallas is therefore a textual 'other' at the beginning of the narrative because of her refusal to be confined within socially acceptable parameters for women. One reading of *Stagecoach* deals with Dallas's realignment with the social order.

Reactions from other characters to Dallas define her 'sinful whore' status, notably the Law & Order Women's League (see Style: Sound effects – Musical score) who make Dallas subhuman by referring to her as 'that creature'. Conversely, she is treated as a sexual object by the men in Tonto, who whistle at her suggestively. This 'male admiration' is confined to her sexual status as a prostitute, however, as she is not offered the chivalrous male assistance when boarding the stagecoach, which is offered to Mrs Mallory as a further social status classification.

Dallas's bravery is highlighted at this juncture, and it is significant that she admits that she is cast as a social 'other' almost on a level with the Apache Indians. As the party is warned by army representatives about the danger of their route, Dallas murmurs 'There are worse things than Apaches.' The corresponding shot of disapproving glances from the Law & Order League women functions as a textual criticism on how social respectability is not always equated with 'natural goodness'. The viewer is encouraged more and more to share Dallas's views because of the 'good' status she is gradually granted.

While Mrs Mallory is constantly consulted about her preferences at the first stop, Dallas is ignored. It is noteworthy that Ringo reprimands Hatfield for his obvious refusal to extend conventional courtesy to Dallas, thereby highlighting the division between the two female types. Dallas is a social outcast in this stopover meal scene and is aligned with Ringo as a result, as he equally resists socially respectable categorisation. Mrs Mallory's refusal to sit with Dallas and the other travellers' refusal to acknowledge her presence serve to define Dallas and Ringo physically as 'other'.

The change in the presentation of Dallas from 'sinful whore' to 'natural wife and mother' is significant in this scene as she becomes increasingly defined in relation to Ringo and his textual heroic status. The shot reverse shots evident in this scene between Dallas and Ringo are a film grammar indicator of a romantic exchange. The sharing of looks and knowledge between Dallas and Ringo, which the reader decodes, suggests a shared romantic understanding and mutual respect. The Hays Production Code institutional enforcement is important here, because just as Mrs Mallory's pregnancy or confinement cannot be textually represented, so a frank display of physical affection is not permissible (see Production history).

The second stop which is marked by Mrs Mallory's confinement, is the background of Dallas's assertion of her 'good female' textual authority. Her unfettered sexuality and sinful status become eroded because of her actions and representation.

Alongside Doc's recovery of self-respect (see Character representation, Doc Boone, above) and renewal of professional respectability as the result of his successful delivery of Mrs Mallory's baby, Dallas is granted equal textual status. She actively helps to deliver the baby and becomes established as a 'natural mother and homemaker'. Dallas is unable to occupy either role legitimately at this narrative point, for obvious reasons, but Mrs Mallory's helplessness and the need to supply the men with food open textual possibilities for altering Dallas's status.

Dallas's emergence with Mrs Mallory's baby presents a 'Madonna with child' image, and evokes silent awe in the men (see Filmography: Intertextual motifs). The romantic exchanges between Dallas and Ringo mediated through camera shots serve to redefine her status as a potential nurturing wife and mother possessing social properties desirable in a woman, rather than as the earlier sexual object.

Ringo and Dallas discover a shared 'other' status in that they both are orphans, which offers an explanation for their removal from mainstream society. Ringo has acted on the wrong side of the social law and Dallas as a prostitute has forfeited the status of a 'lady'. The romantic courtship between them is based on a ranch utopia, which follows the Western values of home making within the 'natural environment' outside the city's norms and values of Mrs Mallory and Hatfield (see Style: Set design and setting).

The text departs therefore from subscribing to the didactic social order adhered to by the Law & Order League, but opts for an alternative civilisation which is based on 'natural decency and goodness'. The dominant white patriarchal ideology is still enforced, however, in the expulsion of the Apache Indians in order for white men to 'claim' their homesteads, and in women becoming defined in relation to a male by subscribing to the socially acceptable role of wife and mother.

Dallas is first seen to be given patriarchal protection by Ringo when discussing her orphan status and the consequences it had for her future. His comment on her loss of her family being hard 'especially on a girl' serves as a textual reminder of women's frailty which cannot compare with male independence.

Ringo's masculinity allows him to cope more easily with the hardships he encounters, and he remains an individual as a result. Dallas's individual status is negated at the expense of social categorisation. She is a 'sinful whore' in social terms who is unable to receive salvation because she is not respectfully opting for the 'natural' choices of wife and mother. The scene in which Dallas is prepared to sacrifice herself, urging Ringo to escape, serves as a reminder of this for the viewer. Dallas obviously wants to choose the life on the ranch which Ringo can offer her because she is aware that the future for women of her status is bleak. Ringo offers salvation based on mutual affection and an opportunity to turn away from her present profession.

Self-recognition from the 'sinful whore' is a powerful textual means to reinforce a preferred institutional representation of women because the viewer is urged to sympathise with the character. If Dallas exchanges her sexual status for that of a wife and mother, the binary opposition of being defined in relation to a man is made to appear the 'natural choice'.

When the party resume travel for the final phase of their journey, Dallas's metamorphosis from 'sinful whore' to 'natural heroine' is realised. The narrative crisis point is reached when the party face attack by the Apache Indians. Dallas's actions are wholly selfless, as seen in the protection she affords to Mrs Mallory's baby. Though without a child of her own, Dallas is identified here with the protective maternal role, as she is shown cradling the baby and concerned only with its welfare.

Dallas still has to confess to Ringo that she is a prostitute. On reaching Lordsburg, Dallas's 'sinful whore' status is revealed through the mise-en-scène. She becomes identified with the saloon, or brothel, to which she goes after safely depositing Mrs Mallory's baby. She is reluctant to marry Ringo because of her position as a 'fallen woman'. Her sins are absolved through Ringo's recognition that she is an innately 'good person', and through the patriarchal protection he can offer her, the ranch utopia becomes reality as Dallas and Ringo ride into the sunset.

FEMALE REPRESENTATION AND HOLLYWOOD

The representation of women in *Stagecoach* is based on an established Hollywood convention, namely that of the 'divided woman' which is most usefully explored through binary oppositions. The phrase 'divided woman' refers to categorising women's on-screen representation into types. Hollywood's 'stable star system' in which male and female stars alike are defined as types and groomed for genres rather like thoroughbred racehorses, bred a casting strategy in which once a star becomes renowned for possessing certain characteristics – such as physical appearance or acting style – their positioning within the narrative and the audience

character representation

perception of them often remain static. The star is given a stock role and repeats the performance with slight variations of character and narrative situation (see Background: Key players' biographies).

Studio and audience associations simultaneously confer on a star the 'hero', 'heroine', 'femme fatale', 'villain' status. Part of the audience's pleasure in the genre lies in predicting the star's place within the narrative structure.

Stagecoach is a highly interesting text to analyse in relation to women because it challenges and reinforces the dominant ideology in female representation. The reinforcement of dominant ideological concerns is evident in the stark oppositions in the presentation of Mrs Mallory and of Dallas.

Dallas's increased narrative status and 'natural goodness' undermine Mrs Mallory textually by the narrative's close to challenge 'civilised perceptions of femininity'. Arguably, this is cosmetic, however, as the wider concerns of women being defined in relation to a man and their 'pre-ordained' role as wife and mother are reinforced in the closing union between Ringo and Dallas and final narrative equilibrium.

Historically women were particularly susceptible to cross-cultural stereotyping, which reflects longstanding literary, theatrical and social traditions which cast females as 'types'. Institutionally, Hollywood was at this stage controlled by the WASP (White Anglo-Saxon Protestant, and, by implication, male) sensibility of the studio executives who managed women's status within films by defining them in relation to male social perceptions.

The Apache Indians and women can be both be interpreted by the viewer as textual others The difference in status between these two groups, in which women are afforded a 'higher hierarchical positioning' is based on ethnicity owing to the 'white' status of the women who quite literally in Mrs Mallory's case exist to ensure the continuation of a white American family and maintain the status quo.

Binary opposition representation can be linked to institutional ideology because the text offers a preferred reading on the 'type' of woman which is socially acceptable. This is of course 'the respectable mother and

women in the Western

homemaker' because it subscribes to a dominant American patriarchal ideology which defines women in relation to men.

The 'sinful whore' character must be expelled from the narrative by the closing equilibrium ensuring that the overt sexuality of women existing outside their relationships with men will be controlled. It is perceived to be a dangerous quality for women because it offers power and pleasure outside the dutiful role of wife and mother which operates in relation to social male desires rather than their own. This is why women are conferred the 'other' status because they are incapable of being textually defined outside the parameters of 'white male social order'.

REPRESENTATION OF WOMEN IN THE WESTERN

The Western genre has evolved so that the hero faces an additional narrative threat in the shape of a woman. If the hero is tempted by the woman then his quest becomes threatened and the final narrative equilibrium is threatened. This attitude reflects the universal treatment of women historically. Hamlet's line to Ophelia, 'Frailty, thy name is woman', might have been tailormade for the Western. Ringo is tempted away from fulfilling his heroic quest to avenge the killing of his family by the Plummer brothers. He must accomplish his heroic quest (see Narrative & Form: Narrative theory) before he can marry Dallas. When close to escaping at a stopover Ringo sees the smoke signals which function as a warning and prevent him from giving up his initial intentions.

This textual example serves to demonstrate the danger of men relying too much on female advice. If Ringo had listened to Dallas's pleas, his masculine function as avenger within the narrative would have been threatened. Dallas must be defined in relation to Ringo and his wishes.

cultural contexts

INTERTEXTUAL NARRATIVE STRANDS

Stagecoach contains two established narrative strands which intertextually draw on existing forms. The prologue establishes the first strand which is developed around the Apache Indian threat to the stagecoach party.

The story of a journey through dangerous terrain is one of the oldest narrative themes in world literature. It forms the basis of *The Odyssey*, as well as of medieval romances such as *The Faerie Queene*. The link between this tradition and *Stagecoach* is recognised and discussed by Edward Buscombe in his *Stagecoach* (p. 24). The picaresque element of the text can be linked with eighteenth-century literary trends developed by Henry Fielding in his novels *Joseph Andrews* and *Tom Jones*.

These instances serve to demonstrate that the simple plot strand of taking a potentially perilous journey is a traditional narrative form to be found in oral culture, print and moving image alike. It provides much scope for adventure and audience participation. In terms of the broad audience appeal of *Stagecoach*, the picaresque functions particularly effectively, because it provides a plausible plot drawing seemingly disparate characters together.

The second narrative strand to which *Stagecoach* is indebted, links with the Proppian narrative theory about myths and the hero fulfilling a particular quest (see Narrative & Form: Narrative theory). The revenge quest too is a traditional theme, often present in Renaissance drama and the Victorian melodrama.

The revenge quest is pursued because of the hero's personal sense of honour which drives him to avenge a wrong. Ringo summarises his own personal compulsion for revenge: 'There are some things a man just can't run away from.' The threat he faces through being branded a common criminal by society is unimportant in relation to his own drive to right the family wrong.

Hatfield, in comparison, runs away from the enemy in a crisis, and Gatewood is literally running away as a criminal under the socially respectable guise of a gentleman. They are revelatory foils to Ringo, proving once again the Fordian maxim that appearances can be deceptive.

cultural contexts contexts

INTERTEXTUAL CASTING

The casting of Berton Churchill, a former New York union leader, functions as a signifier for the contemporary audience of *Stagecoach* (see Background: Key players' biographies). Churchill had a reputation for his portrayals of socially respectable individuals with professional status who are shown to be self-seeking and conceited, or, in this textual instance, corrupt and deceitful. Gatewood's occupation as banker links him with the fast expanding commercial economy as is shown in his remark: 'What's good for the banks is good for the country.'

Ford aligns his banker with generic counterparts who are rarely offered a respectful or laudable Western status. There is a historical point worth making here, that retrospective accounts tend to blame eastern capitalists for the hardships which befell the small Western farmers in the nineteenth century. There is a link here with Ringo who, as a landholder himself, is threatened by Gatewood. Ford has his revenge by exposing the 'money hungry' Gatewood as a common criminal.

Intertextual casting serves the larger purpose of giving Ford the scope to criticise aspects of American society within a studio organised generic form. This consolidates further his directorial status as auteur (see Background: Director as auteur).

Gatewood's tirades are shown through his final narrative status as common crook to be dramatically ironic: 'I don't know what the government's coming to. Instead of protecting businessmen it pokes its nose into business. Why, they're even talking now about having bank examiners. As if we bankers don't know how to run our own banks.' Gatewood is obliquely criticising here the programme of Franklin D. Roosevelt's New Deal, which was being implemented at the time.

Ford returns to his own mythical construction of the American West to question contemporary concerns. The rationale for this is partly his desire to avoid a contentious overly didactic approach. Ideological instruction is preferably disseminated under the guise of mass popular entertainment in which Hollywood excels.

Within this framework Ford does employ some textual subversion about the 'other' status of Ringo and Dallas. In the consolidation of the final

filmography

equilibrium it is textually commendable that they are out of step with established gentlemanly opinions and actions (or lack of) espoused by Hatfield and Gatewood. These two are exposed as, respectively, a rhetorical coward, ill-equipped to offer in practical terms the theoretical protection he promises Lucy, and a common crook dressed up in socially acceptable attire.

This links with Ford's background and again with the personal viewpoint he imposes on a popular generic form. Working within an established dominant ideology of Hollywood did not prevent him circumventing its norms and values as shown by his shrewd use of types like Hatfield and Gatewood. Independence of mind which he instilled in his inspiration, Wayne, is mirrored in his own life. This is illustrated by his $1000 contribution for the Loyalists in the Spanish Civil War towards an ambulance fund. Ford, himself a Catholic, resisted the American Catholic establishment's support of Franco. Ford demonstrates himself worthy of the auteur mantle in that he worked within the establishment of Hollywood to express anti-establishment views.

In 1937, a letter to his nephew Bob Ford validates this view. 'Politically, I am a definite socialist democrat – always left.' This is in contrast to the traditionally right-wing capitalist roots of Hollywood.

filmography: intertextual motifs

Stagecoach established Monument Valley as a vital signifier of the Western genre. It plays an important part in *Stagecoach* and in subsequent Fordian Westerns. Monument Valley has by now become a cliché. Spaghetti Western films such as *The Good, the Bad and the Ugly*, sought to reinvent the genre in the late 1960s–1970s by shooting in Almeria, Spain, and introducing a more subtropical locale.

Recently, however, film directors such as Ridley Scott have acknowledged their own intertextual debt to Monument Valley. This is demonstrated in Scott's *Thelma and Louise* (1991) which draws on the intertextual motif of

Monument Valley but for a more contemporary effect. The text which relates two women's 'escape for the weekend' from domestic servitude into an unexpected Western adventure revises women's positioning in a Hollywood film (see Character representation: Female representation and Hollywood).

Rewriting the Western with 'cowgirls', 'Cadillac', and paying homage to Ford's natural environment the genre is revitalised via the road movie. Arguably, road movies, which include *Bonnie and Clyde* (1967) and *Butch Cassidy and the Sundance Kid* (1969) as classic textual examples, draw on Ford's Western routes. *Bonnie and Clyde* instils the gangster genre with the wonder of the open road instead of the traditional urban confines of the dark sinister city. Similarly, *Butch Cassidy and the Sundance Kid* suggests in its title cowboy protagonists whose adventures come to them on the open road.

The longevity of the Western can be traced outside Hollywood film in a variety of counter-institutional contexts. This shows that the genre has the fluidity to be incorporated within a hybrid generic structure, as *Stagecoach* itself illustrates.

Furthermore, it can be rewritten in a different cultural context. Interesting contemporary 'takes' centre in the rewritten form on the traditional 'other'. By taking a genre which has traditionally oppressed a particular group, for example, women, *Thelma and Louise* rewrites and repositions the narrative conventions. Rather like the Ringo Kid being granted textual authority when he takes the reins of the stagecoach and saves the day, Thelma and Louise are empowered because unlike Mrs Mallory and Dallas they are not merely passengers in a stagecoach but own and drive a car. They are agents of action rather than passive recipients of fate and male activity.

Neo-religious allegory: *Stagecoach* also draws on religious symbolism to position its readers to distinguish between 'goodness' and 'badness' (see Character representation, above). Ford's approach towards Catholicism is traditional in some respects, notably in his treatment of women and the binary opposition strategy preferred by Hollywood. The concept of sin and redemption is less orthodox in *Stagecoach*, however, evidenced by the 'real Christians' on whom Ford chooses to confer his directorial blessing in the closing narrative. The social outcasts are shown to the viewer to be richer for living the life they choose. The drunk, the prostitute and the outlaw are offered redemption and demonstrate the greatest charity throughout the text. Sanctimonious pride is shown to be the greatest sin, particularly for those of Southern origins, as Hatfield's narrative fate testifies.

genre

C. McArthur (see Kerr, P. (ed.), *The Hollywood Film Industry*, Introduction, p. 20) argues that the Western and the gangster film are two major Hollywood film genres which are inextricably linked to America. Generically, they have developed codes and conventions, and a specific iconography enables America to be represented in a mythic form (see Narrative & Form: Narrative theory).

THE WESTERN GENRE AND HOLLYWOOD

Contemporary urban genres predominated in Hollywood during the 1930s. The gangster genre was strengthening Warner Bros' studio status, and audiences were revelling in the representation of the present. Wisecracking urban heroes, notably Jimmy Cagney and Humphrey Bogart, appealed to the sensibilities of an audience who could relate to the 'ordinary guy done good'. Despite the narrative closure which punished the gangster for his flagrant disrespect of the law, the predominant interest for an audience was in following his rise which often poked fun at the establishment.

The Western had to fight back against contemporary preoccupations to regain popularity, and *Stagecoach* achieved this by enriching a retrospective setting with well-drawn characters and universal thematic concerns. Dirk (see p. 20) regards the text as seminal not only for securing Ford's and Wayne's pivotal power positions in Hollywood but also for elevating the form of this genre. A successful genre depends on its ability to remain current for the audience it serves (see Cultural contexts, above) and Ford's indictment of morality and humanity in the film gave the Western and *Stagecoach* a universal appeal. Ford succeeds in using the

Western framework to explore universal human concerns which explains the initial appeal and continuing critical success of *Stagecoach*.

Edward Countryman (see Bell, A., Joyce, M. & Rivers, D., *Advanced Level Media*, p. 220) accurately summarises the appeal of the Western genre which is periodically recycled in American films, albeit in a variety of forms, and retains an enduring interest. 'It is America's preoccupation with the encounter between white America and the continent it has conquered.'

production history

BACKGROUND AND TEXTUAL ORIGINS

Inspired by a story, 'The Stage to Lordsburg', by Ernest Haycox in *Collier's Magazine* in 1937, Ford contacted the author and purchased the film rights for $4000. He later identified Haycox's source for his story as Guy de Maupassant's 'Boule de Suif'. This story centred on a coach journey shared by several prominent citizens and a prostitute travelling through France during the Franco-Prussian war. Ford approached his long-time scriptwriter Dudley Nichols to place the two narrative sources within the Western generic setting and give the characters each their individual style of dialogue and personality.

Ford entrusted Nichols to stress the difference between *Stagecoach* and the B movies by focusing on the traditional appeal of the Western genre. This would be evidenced by dramatic chases exemplified in the eight-minute live action stunt sequence, by the gunfights which take place albeit in a reduced format, and finally, by focusing on impressive scenery, which established Monument Valley as the legendary archetypal Western locale. Nichols was already respected as an established screen writer, as witness his winning the Best Screenplay Oscar for Ford's *The Informer* (1935).

Maupassant's story shares Ford's personal ideological agenda and criticism of society. It mocks the elitist and undeservingly rich bourgeois who bully Boule de Suif. Textual analysis of character function in *Stagecoach* shows Ford levelling his own criticism against American society (see Cultural contexts, above).

The humorous dialogue and well-conceived characters have themselves been immortalised as lasting Western stereotypes. This is particularly evidenced in the variations of the Ringo type which John Wayne has established as the cowboy performance 'blueprint'. The 'tart with the heart' saloon girl epitomised by Dallas has also become a stereotyped female role which Western texts and performances duplicate again and again.

THE EFFECT OF THE 'STAR' SYSTEM

Walter Wanger who effectively greenlighted *Stagecoach* had an established Hollywood reputation as a starmaker. He was credited with discovering famous established studio stars such as Claudette Colbert, Maurice Chevalier and Ginger Rogers.

Claire Trevor was perfectly cast against John Wayne owing to her previous performances which would ensure the necessary audience responses for a sympathetic reading of her role (see Background: Key players' biographies). Critics, notably Edward Buscombe, refer to her mature appearance (although she was only twenty-nine when shooting the film) as a secret of her success in portraying Dallas.

The melodramatic situation of a woman at the crossroads of deciding whether her fate is to grow old as a prostitute or be cast anew as the result of the love of a good man is all the more striking for a viewer.

Conversely, Wayne's casting was based on his youthful looks. Although he was thirty-one years old during shooting, he could easily pass for 'the kid' owing to Trevor appearing older than he. Wayne was Ford's first choice for Ringo. Ford had met Wayne ten years earlier when he was working as a 'prop boy'.

Wayne auditioned for Ford in 1937 and startled the director by nearly talking himself out of a ground-breaking job by suggesting Lloyd Nolan as a sound alternative. Incredulous, Ford retorted, 'Damn you, Duke, can't you do it?'

Wayne agreed to perform in the film, which presented Ford with the final difficulty of selling his key role choice to any of the Hollywood studios. Walter Wanger was appealed to, who preferred that Gary Cooper play the Ringo Kid. Ford persuaded Wanger as an independent producer to put up $250 000 and allayed his doubts about casting Wayne by assuring him that the picture would lead on the established star name of Claire Trevor. This policy was supported by the publicity strategies which focused on maximising Trevor's star reputation in selling tie-in products.

Tie-in products were associated with star images. Tru-Color Lipstick was produced by Max Factor, and the product promoted in the context of *Stagecoach* supported by a picture of Claire Trevor.

This was a further means to widen the mass appeal of the text to a female audience urging them to identify with and physically emulate the female star by imitating a hairstyle or purchasing a lipstick associated with the film (see Style: Costume and make-up).

AWARDS

In addition to the Oscar won by Thomas Mitchell (Doc Boone), the film was nominated for Best Picture (losing to *Gone with the Wind*), Best Director, Best Black-and-White Cinematography, Best Art Direction/Set Decoration, Best Editing, and Best Score. It won only in the last category (see Style: Sound effects – Musical score). The promotional exposure which the text gained as a result of being nominated for so many Academy awards contributed towards consolidating the reputations of all key players associated with the production.

industrial

Stagecoach took forty-seven working days to shoot, completing photography on 23 December 1938. In those days post-production was speedy. The finished film was ready for preview at the Fox Westwood theatre on 2 February 1939.

Walter Wanger's production role cannot be underestimated. It serves as a reminder of the commercial function of film to which Hollywood has always given priority. Ford was required to justify his production choices to construct a text which would satisfy both himself and his financial backers.

Edward Buscombe in his *Stagecoach* (p. 17) recognises Wanger's pivotal production role as do the opening credits which emblazon 'Walter Wanger presents', in a handwritten script. Wanger's signature as a financial backer is stamped on the film and seals its dual status as a commercial product and a distinguished piece of film making.

Ford's shrewdness and his auteur status are linked to his collaboration with Wanger. Walter Wanger Productions functioned as a branch of United Artists. Wanger is not simply a producer, just as Ford is not simply a director. Wanger was acutely aware of popular commercial trends (see Production history, above) but was capable of risk-taking independence. *Stagecoach* was no exception, providing financial dividends aplenty but also setting trends for the genre and establishing key players, notably John Wayne (see Background: Key players' biographies).

SHOOTING ON LOCATION

On gaining the greenlight Ford assembled a cast and crew of eighty-five people in Monument Valley. Other location sites included the towns of Kernville, Victorville, Fremont Pass, Calabasas, Chatsworth California and Dry Lake in Utah and Colorado. The location was seminal as no film had ever been shot in Monument Valley, notorious for its arid climate and remoteness. The valley proved an audience draw owing to its sheer vastness and the novelty of using it as a screen location.

Ford established the potential of deep focus camera work in his location shoot which included shots of the stagecoach taken from forty miles' distance away from the moving coach. The ten-week shoot was accompanied by a three-month post production phase in which the film was edited and musically scored.

CODES OF CONDUCT AND CENSORSHIP

Link to Hays Production Code: Ford's auteur status did not grant him exemption from the pervasive Hays Production Code which can be traced in the representation of characters and treatment of adult relationships (see Character representation, above).

A striking comparison can be drawn between the inspirational source of the film, 'Boule de Suif', which, written in 1880, is franker in its treatment of prostitution than *Stagecoach*, produced some fifty-eight years later. Dallas is never referred to as a prostitute. The film grammar and her relations with other characters must suggest this key fact by implication (see Character representation, above).

Treatment of romance between Ringo and Dallas: The romance between Ringo and Dallas is denied actual representation on screen. It is deliberately muted, a quick embrace favoured above the traditional romantic kiss. This links to censorship guidelines during this period which prevent Dallas from being revered as a 'romantic icon' owing to her 'impure profession'.

Representation of violence: The short shootout is also directly related to the influence of the Hays Production Code. The evil character of the Plummer brothers is suggested by their menacing glances. Their violent reputation is implied by the newspaper hoardings for the next day being prepared in advance. The deft shootout shows how censorship prevented violence being represented or glamorised. As a generic convention, however, it is vital that Ford retains the shootout. It has a vital secondary narrative function enabling Ringo to complete his heroic quest (see Narrative & Form: Narrative theory). In Westerns the final equilibrium must always be enforced by a climactic act of violence performed by the good cowboy protecting the Western frontier, threatened in this instance by a corrupt civilisation and the Apache Indians.

MARKETING OF THE FILM

A pressbook was released which detailed a comprehensive selection of textual promotional products. Exhibitors could send for tie-ins including bookmarks and novelty Western hats. To broaden the potential mass audience, the film was translated into other media allowing dissemination, including a variety of publicity channels. Radio stations could obtain a fifteen-minute disc. Print media included a five thousand word newspaper serialisation and a photostory version. A fifteen-minute dramatised script was further produced for school based performances.

audience

The complexity of *Stagecoach* affords a variety of interpretations for the reader. James Halloran's remark concerning 'what people do with the media' (see Bell, A., Joyce, M. & Rivers, D., *Advanced Level Media*, p. 78) provides food for thought in making sweeping assumptions about the audience reception process.

The preferred readings identified in earlier discussion (see Ideology, above) can be textually corroborated, but *Stagecoach* might provide aberrant readings.

An example of this is the female audience who might use Dallas as a role model of feminine empowerment. Despite her final narrative subservience, it can equally be argued that she finds a harmonious utopia on equal terms with the man she loves and outside the world of the brothel which she despises. Similarly, her textual action confirms her status as a heroine, and the top billing Claire Trevor received at the time made her a key figure associated with the text. Charges of misogyny levelled against Ford and his auteur intentions become redundant therefore in an alternative feminine reading of this nature.

CRITICAL ACCOUNTS

The extracts given below indicate the range of responses which *Stagecoach* has generated. *Stagecoach* functions as a seminal text in illustrating many elements of André Bazin's theory.

> By the eve of the war the Western had reached a definitive stage of perfection. The year 1940 marks a point beyond which some new development seemed inevitable, a development that the four years of war delayed, then modified, though without controlling it. *Stagecoach* (1939) is the ideal example of the maturity of a style brought to classical perfection. John Ford struck the ideal balance between social myth, historical reconstruction, psychological truth and the traditional theme of the Western mise en scène. None of these elements dominated any other. *Stagecoach* is like a wheel, so perfectly made that it remains in equilibrium on its axis in any position.
>
> *André Bazin, What is Cinema? Vol II, quoted by Edward Buscombe in Stagecoach, p. 85*

Bazin's location of *Stagecoach* within a hybrid textual status:

> After the war Bazin maintained, a mutation set in, a development towards something he called the 'superwestern': 'a Western that

audience

would be ashamed to be just itself, and looks for some additional interest to justify its existence – an aesthetic, sociological, moral, psychological, political or erotic interest, in short some quality extrinsic to the genre and which is supposed to enrich it.'

Edward Buscombe, Stagecoach, p. 85

REVIEWS

The Motion Picture Herald of 11 February 1939 rated the film 'a solid and soundly satisfying demonstration of the virtue inherent in the entertainment-for-entertainment's-sake policy of film production, gripping in universal appeal, spectacular in photographic beauty'.

Photoplay of 4 April 1939 called it '*Grand Hotel* on wheels' and was full of praise for Wayne's 'attractive and sincere performance'.

A. Jympson Harman in *The Evening News* of 9 June 1939: 'This is a great film – the kind that gets itself into the movie history books.'

C.A. Lejeune in *The Observer* of 11 June 1939: 'One of the most exciting experiences the cinema has brought us.'

Dilys Powell in *The Sunday Times* of 11 June 1939: 'One of the most exciting Westerns I have seen for years.'

Cinebooks Reviews: The classic western, *Stagecoach* is John Ford's greatest epic of the frontier. This western eclipsed all films in the genre that had gone before it and so vastly influenced those that followed that its stamp can be found in most superior westerns made since Ford stepped into Monument Valley for the first time. With the exception of his abortive leap into leading man status in *The Big Trail* (1930), John Wayne had been languishing on the tiny backlots of Poverty Row studios, riding through a host of forgettable B westerns until summoned by Ford to fame, fortune, and stardom in this film.

Stagecoach, set in a landscape of endless horizons, is a wonderful broad portrait of pioneer life in the untamed Great SouthWest, as well as an in-depth character study of eight people, all diverse in their pursuits and all traveling to separate fates on a journey packed with danger.

Cinemania 96, CD ROM, Microsoft Corporation

bibliography

general film

Altman, Rick, *Film Genre*,
BFI, 1999
  Detailed exploration of film genres

Bordwell, David, *Narration in the
Fiction Film*, Routledge, 1985
  A detailed study of narrative theory
  and structures

– – –, Staiger, Janet & Thompson,
Kristin, *The Classical Hollywood
Cinema: Film Style & Mode of
Production to 1960*, Routledge, 1985;
pprbk 1995
  An authoritative study of cinema as
  institution, it covers film style and
  production

– – – & Thompson, Kristin, *Film Art*,
McGraw-Hill, 4th edn, 1993
  An introduction to film aesthetics for
  the non-specialist

Branson, Gill & Stafford, Roy, *The
Media Studies Handbook*, Routledge,
1996

Buckland, Warren, *Teach Yourself
Film Studies*, Hodder & Stoughton,
1998
  Very accessible, it gives an overview
  of key areas in film studies

Cook, Pam (ed.), *The Cinema Book*,
British Film Institute, 1994

Corrigan, Tim, *A Short Guide To
Writing About Film*,
HarperCollins, 1994
  What it says: a practical guide for
  students

Dyer, Richard, *Stars*, London BFI,
1979
  A good introduction to the star
  system

Easthope, Antony, *Classical Film
Theory*, Longman, 1993
  A clear overview of recent writing
  about film theory

Hayward, Susan, *Key Concepts in
Cinema Studies*,
Routledge, 1996

Hill, John & Gibson, Pamela Church
(eds), *The Oxford Guide to Film Studies*,
Oxford, 1998
  Wide-ranging standard guide

Lapsley, Robert & Westlake, Michael,
Film Theory: An Introduction,
Manchester University Press, 1994

Maltby, Richard & Craven, Ian,
Hollywood Cinema,
Blackwell, 1995
  A comprehensive work on the
  Hollywood industry and its
  products

Mulvey, Laura, 'Visual Pleasure and
Narrative Cinema' (1974), in *Visual
and Other Pleasures*,
Indiana University Press, Bloomington,
1989
  The classic analysis of 'the look' and
  'the male gaze' in Hollywood cinema.
  Also available in numerous other
  edited collections

Nelmes, Jill (ed.),
Introduction to Film Studies,
Routledge, 1996
  Deals with several national cinemas
  and key concepts in film study

Nowell-Smith, Geoffrey (ed.),
The Oxford History of World Cinema,
Oxford, 1996
  Hugely detailed and wide-ranging
  with many features on 'stars'

general film bibliography

Thomson, David, **A Biographical Dictionary of the Cinema**, Secker & Warburg, 1975
Unashamedly driven by personal taste, but often stimulating

Truffaut, François, **Hitchcock**, Simon & Schuster, 1966, rev. edn, Touchstone, 1985
Landmark extended interview

Turner, Graeme, **Film as Social Practice**, 2nd edn, Routledge, 1993
Chapter four, 'Film Narrative', discusses structuralist theories of narrative

Wollen, Peter, **Signs and Meaning in the Cinema**, Viking, 1972
An important study in semiology

Readers should also explore the many relevant websites and journals. *Film Education* and *Sight and Sound* are standard reading.

Valuable websites include:

The Internet Movie Database at http://uk.imdb.com

Screensite at http://www.tcf.ua.edu/screensite/contents.html

The Media and Communications Site at the University of Aberystwyth at http://www.aber.ac.uk/~dgc/welcome.html

There are obviously many other university and studio websites which are worth exploring in relation to film studies.

stagecoach

Anderson, Lindsay, **About John Ford**, Plexus, London, 1981

Baxter, John, **The Cinema of John Ford**, Zwemmer, 1971

Bazin, André, **What is Cinema?** Vol. II (Translated by Hugh Gray), University of California Press, Berkeley, 1971

Bell, Angela, Joyce, Mark & Rivers, Danny, **Advanced Level Media**, Hodder & Stoughton, 1999

Bogdanovich, Peter, **John Ford**, Studio Vista, 1967

Box Office, Review of *Stagecoach*, 11 February 1939

Buscombe, Edward (ed.), **The BFI Companion to the Western**, BFI/André Deutsch, 1988

– – – (ed.), **The BFI Companion to the Western**, Da Capo Press, New York, 1991

– – – **Stagecoach**, BFI, 1992

Caughie, John, **Theories of Authorship**, BFI, 1981

Dayan, Daniel, **Western Graffiti**, Editions Clancier-Guénaud, Paris, 1983

Everson, William, **The Hollywood Western**, Citadel Press, New York, 1992

Folsom, James K., **The Western: A Collection of Critical Essays**, Prentice-Hall, Inc., 1979

Ford, Dan, **Pappy: The Life of John Ford**, Prentice-Hall, 1979

Frayling, Christopher, **Spaghetti Westerns: Cowboys and Europeans from Karl May to Sergio Leone**, Routledge & Kegan Paul, 1981

Gallagher, Tag, **John Ford; The Man and his Films**, University of California Press, Berkeley, 1986

Gassner, John & Nichols, Dudley (eds), *Great Film Plays*, Crown Publishers, Inc., New York, 1959

Hardy, Phil, *Encyclopaedia of the Western*, Aurum Press, 1987

– – – *The Western*, Aurum Press, 1983

Harman, A. Jympson, Review of *Stagecoach*, *The Evening News*, 9 June 1939

Harte, F. Bret, 'The Outcasts of Poker Flat', in *Overland Monthly and Out West Magazine*, Vol. 2, issue 1, San Francisco, January 1869

Henderson, B., 'The Searchers: An American Dilemma', in B. Nichols (ed.), *Movies and Methods*, Vol.2, University of California Press, London, 1985

Kaplan, E. Ann (ed.), *Women in Film Noir*, BFI, 1989

Kerr, Paul (ed.), Introduction, *The Hollywood Film Industry*, Routledge & Kegan Paul, 1986

Kitses, Jim, *Horizons West*, Thames and Hudson, 1969

– – – *Horizons West*, Studio Vista, 1972

Lejeune, C.A., Review of *Stagecoach*, *The Observer*, 11 June 1939

Leutrat, Jean-Louis & Liandrat-Guignes, Suzanne, *Les Cartes de l'Ouest*, Armand Colin, Paris, 1990

McBride, Joseph & Wilmington, Mike, *John Ford*, Secker & Warburg, 1974

Miller, Don, *Hollywood Corral*, Popular Library, New York, 1976

Mitchell, Lee Clark, *Westerns: Making the Man in Fiction and Film*, University of Chicago Press, 1994

Mitry, Jean, *John Ford*, Editions Universitaires, Paris, 1954

Monaco, James, *How to Read a Film*, Oxford University Press, 1981

Motion Picture Herald, The, Review of *Stagecoach*, 11 February 1939

Murdoch, David H., 'The Western Myth', *The Listener*, 10 January 1985

Neale, Steve, 'Questions of Genre', *Screen*, Vol.31, No.1, 1990

Nugent, Frank S., Review of *Stagecoach*, *New York Times*, 3 March 1939

Photoplay, Review of *Stagecoach*, 4 April 1939

Pirie, David (ed.), *Anatomy of the Movies*, Windward, London, 1981

Place, J.A., *The Western Films of John Ford*, Citadel Press, New York, 1975

Powell, Dilys, Review of *Stagecoach*, *The Sunday Times*, 11 June 1939

Pumphrey, Martin, 'Why Do Cowboys Wear Hats in the Bath?', *Critical Quarterly*, Vol.31, No.3, 1988

Pye, Douglas, '*The Searchers* and Teaching the Industry', *Screen Education*, No.17, 1972

Sinclair, Andrew, *John Ford; A Biography*, Dial Press, New York, 1979

Tompkins, Jane, *West of Everything: The Inner Life of Westerns*, Oxford University Press, New York, 1992

Variety, Review of *Stagecoach*, 8 February 1939

Warshow, Robert, *The Immediate Experience*, Anchor Books, New York, 1964

Wright, Will, *Sixguns and Society: A Structural Study of the Western*, University of California Press, Berkeley, 1975

filmography

Recommended John Ford texts to analyse in terms of auteur status and directorial canon:

Outcasts of Poker Flat, The (1919) (John Ford as Jack Ford)

Iron Horse, The (1924) John Ford

Three Bad Men (1926) John Ford

Dr Bull (1933) John Ford

Judge Priest (1934) John Ford

Informer, The (1935) John Ford

Steamboat 'Round The Bend (1935) John Ford

Prisoner of Shark Island, The (1936) John Ford

Drums along the Mohawk (1939) John Ford

Stagecoach (1939) John Ford

Young Mr Lincoln (1939) John Ford

Grapes of Wrath, The (1940) John Ford

Long Voyage Home, The (1940) John Ford

My Darling Clementine (1946) John Ford

Fort Apache (1948) John Ford

She Wore a Yellow Ribbon (1949) John Ford

Rio Grande (1950) John Ford

Wagon Master (1950) John Ford

Quiet Man, The (1952) John Ford

Searchers, The (1956) John Ford

Wings of Eagles, The (1957) John Ford

Man Who Shot Liberty Valance, The (1962) John Ford

Cheyenne Autumn (1964) John Ford

Seven Women (1966) John Ford

Comparative 1930s text representing urbanisation:

Angels with Dirty Faces (1938) Michael Curtiz

Contemporary recommended 'New Hollywood' text which features negative representation of urbanisation:

Seven (1995) David Fincher

Comparative Westerns to analyse textually alongside Stagecoach in terms of ideology, generic codes and conventions, and representational issues:

Battle of Elderbush Gulch, The (1914) D.W. Griffith

Code of the West (1925) J.P. McGowan

Destry Rides Again (1939) George Marshall

Jesse James (1939) Henry King

Geronimo (1939) Paul H. Sloane

Oklahoma Kid, The (1939) Lloyd Bacon

Rio Bravo (1959) Howard Hawks

True Grit (1969) Henry Hathaway

Developmental genre text in establishing the 'spaghetti Western':

The Good, The Bad and The Ugly (1966) Sergio Leone

Hybrid genre Western texts meriting viewing because they demonstrate how the Western genre has evolved post-Stagecoach:

Bonnie and Clyde (1967) Arthur Penn

Butch Cassidy and the Sundance Kid (1969) George Roy Hill

Shootist, The (1976) Don Siegel

Thelma and Louise (1991) Ridley Scott

filmography

Remakes of *Stagecoach* which merit textual comparison:

Stagecoach (1966) Gordon Douglas

Stagecoach (1986) Ted Post

Seminal Orson Welles texts which demonstrate the 1940s celluloid practice of developing deep focus techniques pioneered and deployed in *Stagecoach*:

Citizen Kane (1941) Orson Welles

Magnificent Ambersons, The (1942) Orson Welles

Recommended 'New Hollywood' text which represents a 'masculine ideal' of the action hero which can be compared with John Wayne's established status as an 'action star' in the Western genre:

Die Hard (1988) George McTiernan

Recommended 'film noir' text which illustrates female binary opposition:

Double Indemnity (1944) Billy Wilder

cinematic terms

180-degree system according to this established Hollywood classical narrative convention, the space of any scene is constructed along an axis, the 180-degree line. In order to ensure that the audience maintains its bearings and spatial orientation, the shooting camera must always stay on the same side of the imaginary line

aberrant reading decoding of a text which differs from the preferred reading intended by the director. These are often individual textual readings

auteur the director as prime author of a film employing a recognisable style

B movie a film which has a lower status than its 'A' grade counterpart. B movies usually form part of the overall cinema feature bill with the main event, the headlining picture, receiving top billing

binary opposition a structuralist term which demonstrates how meaning can be constructed through the deliberate contrasts between two representations. By creating two different character types the properties of both become separate and interestingly incapable of coexistence. Female representation as a result is simplified as is the textual positioning of women who are either an 'other' or a protagonist

celluloid an alternative term for film or film stock

character actor actor who concentrates on the in-depth construction of character. Character actors gain a reputation for their ability to differentiate between separate roles, in contrast to the performance of a star which often relies on external features alone, such as appearance, and physical stature

chiaroscuro from the Italian words for 'clear' and 'dark'. The film practice refers to arranging elements of light and dark to create a celluloid aesthetic effect

cinematography art of making motion pictures, more specifically with regard to lighting and camera work

classical era a period in Hollywood history (roughly between 1935 and 1959) when the studio system was at its peak of popularity and strength. In this era Hollywood established an institutional approach to film production relying on a classic narrative system and studio style

code a system of signs which form a recognisable pattern

connotation association of ideas or meanings which are suggested when interpreting elements of a text systematically

conventions established symbols, motifs, iconography, stock characters or situations which become associated with a particular film genre

decode break down a textual message to make its meaning clear

deconstruction the manner in which a reader interprets a text. Textual deconstruction usually involves breaking down the whole text into a series of elements which create meaning as a result

deep focus cinematography technique which keeps all the elements within a scene in focus

dominant ideology the majority view of what is perceived as ideologically preferable

equilibrium Todorov's term for the opening and closing stasis within a film

cinematic terms

which will be ruptured into disequilibrium at a point of the narrative. The disequilibrium will be succeeded by a final equilibrium by the closure of the narrative

film grammar the visual devices which support a viewer's interpretation of a film text in much the same way that punctuation structures a literary or dramatic text. Example: a specific choice of shot indicating a significant plot development

foil dramatic function which presents meaningful comparisons between characters within a text

form the physical structure of a text

foregrounding focus method of filming by which the background images are less sharp. The subject appears at the front of the shot, thus attracting the viewer's attention

genre a type of film following certain archetypal patterns which define its character, such as the Western, the gangster movie, the science fiction film, or the detective story

green lighting the studio practice of making a film viable by granting production funds and backing to a proposed project at the pre-production stage

Hays Production Code colloquial name for the Motion Picture Producers and Distributors of America Organization, run by Will H. Hays in the 1930s when its Production Code was strictly enforced

hybrid a combination of several features, usually seen as belonging to different genres

iconography the study of images.

Patterns of recognisable images link to a text's generic identification through the associations they provide for a viewer

ideological state apparatus the methods by which a powerful social organisation can enforce an ideological point of view. Hollywood can be seen as playing a mass media role which arguably instils ideology under the guise of popular entertainment forms

ideology a set of beliefs and values which is linked to a dominant power base within a social structure

institutional context specific media organisations exhibit characteristics which can be traced in the media products which they produce. Hollywood can historically be classified as organising its film studios to approach film as a commercial product. This is evidenced by its systems of production, budget allocation and establishment of a star system

intertextual relating to other texts which have recognisably similar content, form or style. Intertextual elements are often used deliberately by text producers to evoke a particular response from the reader

location in cinematography it can be either interior (filmed inside, which can include studio shooting) or exterior (filmed 'on location' at a particular venue outside a manufactured studio set). The term refers to the range of environments which are represented in a text

long shot shooting a subject from a distance. The technique is generally used to encompass a wide range of action, and also to establish the location. It can readily create a sense of space

cinematic terms

melodrama a film (or a play) which exhibits a style which is characterised by an excess of emotion. This is often reflected in a mannered acting style, which involves conscious heightened dialogue delivery. Close-up shots are used to emphasise an emotional state. Music is also introduced as a supporting atmospheric device

mise–en–scène (from the French word 'mise', placing) the phrase means what is placed in a scene, or more specifically how individual film shots are composed

musical motif a recognisable theme tune which is repeated, gaining authority and symbolism within a media text. Musical motifs are often associated with specific characters

myth symbolic use of a narrative form to produce a meaning with a wide general application

narrative the way in which a story is told

negative print print of a film prior to full development and copied cinematic distribution

New Hollywood the industrial renaissance of Hollywood in response to the threatening impact of television. Hollywood revised its approach to film making, notably in the high concept picture and aggressive marketing strategies to define its moving image status as distinct from television and so survive in the contemporary media market place. Historically this can be located in the 1970s, notably with the release of *Jaws*

non diegetic diegetic sound refers to the soundtrack which describes aurally the action of the film. Non diegetic sound refers to a soundtrack, for example an overlaid musical score, which exists outside the world of the film. The soundtrack function in this context is to provide further clarification of the atmosphere or action for the viewer

other the person which is outside and different to the self. Textually 'the self' occupies the prime power position in a text which defines the 'other' in terms of what they are not. Comparisons can be drawn between 'values', 'gender', 'sexuality' and 'ethnicity'

picaresque a narrative which takes the form of a journey undertaken by the protagonist(s)

position the viewer construct a text so as to offer interpretation and comprehension and enable the reader to create a meaning

post production phase the editing, marketing and distribution activities involved in film making

preferred reading the decoding of a text in accordance with the intended meaning created by the text's producer

prologue a narrative scene and context setter which establishes the opening textual situation. It often serves to relay important information

quest a narrative challenge which the hero must overcome. Quests become the stock patterns of certain film genres, linking a series of texts together

reaction shot an inserted shot focusing on a character's reaction to something occurring in the scene. Commonly used to mediate an emotional state

reading a critical close examination of the content of a text as a method of interpreting meaning

STAGECOACH

cinematic terms

realistic aesthetic the practice of film making which strives to approximate realistic conditions, notably in the manner the text is shot

representation the manner in which an individual or group is depicted on screen. Owing to film being institutionally developed, stereotypical representations of groups have become established and repeated in subsequent texts. The study of representation within a film allows critical analysis of why some groups are 'positively' represented and others negatively

shot reverse shot film technique typically used in Hollywood to suggest an exchange of romantic emotion. It involves a single shot of one subject juxtaposed with another subject's reaction. It was used to avoid the restrictions imposed by the Hays Production Code

signifier the conscious deployment of a sign within a text to produce meaning

stock character established type of character which is usually present in a particular narrative, such as a hero or villain. These can vary from one genre to another and in relation to the producer's construction of character

structuralist using an approach to textual analysis which emphasises the structures which comprise the media text being decoded

studio lots large buildings constructed on studio premises which house interior sets

tag-line short written slogan associated with promoting a film text. Tag-lines are useful marketing tools for a film, serving to summarise succinctly a key point associated with the film. They may be related the text's genre or theme

talkies a colloquial term for moving images with sound. Silent and sound films were differentiated by this phrase

text any moving image product which can be read and interpreted by the viewer

textual analysis practice of deconstructing elements which comprise a text so as to consider their particular meaning within the overall textual structure

tie-in products film-related merchandise which functions as an information and promotional tool

credits

production company

Walter Wanger Productions Inc

director

John Ford

producer

Walter Wanger

screenplay

Dudley Nichols

original story

Ernest Haycox

art director

Alexander Toluboff

associate director

Wiard B. Ihnen

director of photography

Bert Glennon

musical director

Boris Morros

musical score based on American folk songs

adapted by Richard Hageman, Franke Harling, Louis Gruenberg, John Leipold, Leo Shuken

cast

Claire Trevor – Dallas

John Wayne – Henry, the Ringo Kid

Andy Devine – Buck, the Stagecoach Driver

John Carradine – Mr Hatfield

Thomas Mitchell – Doc Josiah Boone

Louise Platt – Lucy Mallory

George Bancroft – Curley Wilcox

Donald Meek – Mr Samuel Peacock

Berton Churchill – Mr Elswood Henry Gatewood

Tim Holt – Lieutenant Blanchard

Other titles in the series

Other titles available in the York Film Notes series:

Title	ISBN
8½ (Otto e mezzo)	0582 40488 6
A bout de souffle	0582 43182 4
Apocalypse Now	0582 43183 2
Battleship Potemkin	0582 40490 8
Blade Runner	0582 43198 0
Casablanca	0582 43201 4
Chinatown	0582 43199 9
Citizen Kane	0582 40493 2
Das Cabinet des Dr Caligari	0582 40494 0
Double Indemnity	0582 43196 4
Dracula	0582 43197 2
Easy Rider	0582 43195 6
Fargo	0582 43193 X
Fear Eats the Soul	0582 43224 3
La Haine	0582 43194 8
Lawrence of Arabia	0582 43192 1
Psycho	0582 43191 3
Pulp Fiction	0582 40510 6
Romeo and Juliet	0582 43189 1
Some Like It Hot	0582 40503 3
Taxi Driver	0582 40506 8
The Full Monty	0582 43181 6
The Godfather	0582 43188 3
The Piano	0582 43190 5
The Searchers	0582 40510 6
The Terminator	0582 43186 7
The Third Man	0582 40511 4
Thelma and Louise	0582 43184 0
Unforgiven	0582 43185 9

Also from York Notes

Also available in the **York Notes** range:

York Notes
The ultimate literature guides for GCSE students (or equivalent levels)

York Notes Advanced
Literature guides for A-level and undergraduate students (or equivalent levels)

York Personal Tutors
Personal tutoring on essential GCSE English and Maths topics

Available from good bookshops.
For full details, please visit our website at www.longman-yorknotes.com

STAGECOACH

notes

notes

STAGECOACH